HOW TO MANAGE YOUR HOME & LIFE: TWO BOOKS IN ONE

TIME MANAGEMENT FOR WOMEN + A GUIDE TO DECLUTTERING & ORGANIZING YOUR HOME - HOW TO DECLUTTER & CLEAN HOUSE IN 15 MINUTES - ORGANIZE LIFE DOING LESS

SOPHIE IRVINE

CONTENTS

TIME MANAGEMENT FOR BUSY MOMS

CLUTTER-FREE HOME

TIME MANAGEMENT FOR BUSY MOMS

HOW TO ORGANIZE YOUR LIFE, DO LESS AND GET MORE

INTRODUCTION

We begin to hear the words time management as early as our school years. We begin to learn how to handle home-work, after school activities, and time with our friends. If only life remained as simple as our school days.

Once we reach adulthood, it's like somebody throws a curveball at as. The person we used to be is no longer recog-nizable. There are not enough hours in the day, our families suffer, our work suffers, and the end result is a general feeling of failure.

A lack of time management has a habit of developing into a vicious circle. We get bogged down with our responsibilities, and we end up splitting ourselves in so many directions that each task we attempt to compete is not up to the standard you expect from yourself, leading you to spend more time to get it right.

These tasks aren't just related to our jobs. When I use the term job, this includes being a stay at home mom, a doctor, a writer or a painter. My definition of a job is a task that requires time, be that the ironing or defending a criminal in court.

The problem has become more serious for our generation of females. Many of our great-grandmothers and even grandmothers didn't have to leave home to work nine till five. Their job was to take care of the home and the children.

Some decades ago, mainly after the Second World War, the role of women began to change, and more and more females started joining the workforce. But this left a huge hole in the home. Through nobody's fault, men were just not ready to see their role in the home. This led to moms having two jobs, the one they were paid for, and the one that was still expected of them.

Today, things haven't improved greatly. I don't want anybody reading this thinking that I'm a feminist and this book is going to be about female rights and equality. That is a whole other topic, and debating it isn't going to help solve our issues with time management. But the fact is, many women are struggling with the very real problem of juggling the home, the family and the work commitments.

On a similar note, you are going to read this book from the perspective of a woman. I hope that this is not going to put men off, as there will be a number of tips, tricks, and strategies that can be used by everybody, regardless of their gender.

So What Is the Problem?

Have a look at the typical day of a working mom. She gets up anywhere from 6.30 am to 7 am (assuming the baby hasn't woken her up earlier). She showers, gets dressed and tries to gulp down a look warm coffee in between getting the kids up, dressed, fed and even walking the "family dog". The dishes are washed and possibly even a load of washing on if she's lucky.

By 9 am she has delivered all children to necessary schools and child-care. She opens her emails, begins her day in the office, already the weight of the day's tasks are starting to take their toll. People are asking more and more from her, and she politely says yes, adding things to the list. By 4 pm the list is longer than before and although she hasn't stopped all day, there is an overall feeling that nothing has been done.

She now picks up the children from various school activities and childminders. Sits down and tries to muster up the patience to help them with their homework. By 6.30 pm she remembers the washing that never got hung out, by now it needs rewashing. Husband comes home and looks at the empty kitchen, which is almost enough to start a fight, but there is no time because of the kid's dinner, bathing, stories and bed.

It's 9 pm. The kids are in bed but it's too late for her dinner, her health is now being affected. It should be her time to relax, but the house is quiet, and it's the perfect time to catch up on some work. She is too tired and mistakes are made.

I work from home and the routine can be very similar. Even moms working from home have to structure their day to accommodate for working hours. 6 months ago my life was exactly that of the example. Every day was a long, exhausting chore. There was no pleasure. My daughter was too scared to ask me anything in case it resulted in me blowing a fuse or bursting into tears.

For those that work from home, it can be even worse because it is very difficult to draw a line between your work life and home life. There is no balance, and the endless tasks steal even your weekends.

You just know what's coming next. Arguments begin with your partner. He isn't helping enough. He doesn't know how to put the washing machine on, his idea of contributing to the household chore is cooking, and this normally leaves you with more to clean up.

Some may be reading this and think it's a cliché. It's not. This is a real and very painful problem that many women go through. The feeling of being a complete failure can lead to a lack of sleep, exhaustion, and depression. In the worst-case scenario, it can lead to families being torn apart.

I read many books about time management and how working moms can manage their day to maximize their output. I got lots of ideas, but there wasn't a particular way that that really stuck out and made life-changing differences.

Because of this, I took a step back from my life. I turned the computer off and started going for walks. I felt guilty even for spending 10 minutes away from my responsibilities, and I knew I had to do something.

I banned myself from listening to the success stories of women online. Maybe they did have their whole life in perfect order. The photos on Facebook are always so perfect, and they must be amazing women. This just made me feel worse, not jealous, but incapable of becoming the person I wanted to be.

I knew in my heart that it was going to be impossible to work harder than I was already working. There wasn't a spare minute in the day for me to maximize. It was time for me to implement the 'Do Less, Get More' Strategy.

This book is going to help you, regardless of whether you are a new mom, you have children and you want to start working, you want to begin a business from home, or whether you are literally at your limit and need a solution now.

This strategy worked for me. Even in just a week, I noticed a clearer, happier atmosphere in my home. My partner wanted to be home more. My children were more relaxed, and I finally began to see a balance in my life that I hadn't seen in years.

We are going to put our strategies into place so that you too can see a difference in a matter of days, working towards your perfect life balance in just two weeks.

The first step for you to take is to read this book. I know what is going through your mind; you don't have the time to read it. Yes, you do. I will promise that this book will be lighthearted and fun at the same time as practical and informative. You have to promise to start reading it for 5 minutes a day.

Together, we will work towards doing less and getting more without having to make any sacrifices. And let's start the process by looking at ways we can turn the disorganized chaos into a successful, organized plan.

CHAPTER 1. FROM MESS TO SUCCESS

Discover Yourself: Passion, Goals, What You Want in Life, What Matters.

Before we delve into the techniques of time management, it's important to go back a few steps and start at the basics. We want to make a change, but for the change to be significant and long-lasting, it must be done right. And this is not going to happen overnight.

Now, let's assume that for the next couple of days your life is going to be as hectic as it has been. That doesn't mean that we can't carry out these steps while you are doing your other activities. The first stage is a deep consideration of your life and your objectives.

When I began with this step, I wanted to sit down with pen and paper, but even then I felt too guilty as there were more pressing things to get done. So I used the time I had in between.

It's best to think about your goals and dreams when you are alone, as it's not an activity that should be interrupted. I used my 10 minutes walking the dog or the car journey after dropping off the children. Even that time when you are whizzing around the supermarket can be time for you to engage your brain.

What is it that makes you tick? What do you love? Avoid the obvious answers. Nobody is judging you. We know you love your children and your partner. We know that watching their achievements is the best thing in the world. But right now, you need to go back to you as a person.

For this, I remembered myself in my early 20s. At this stage of my life I wasn't in a serious relationship, nor did I have children. I wasn't somebody's wife or somebody's mom. I was me! This was the time when I felt I could really focus on what was important to me.

There is no coincidence here that at this stage of my life, I also felt that I held things together better. I felt more organized and I was better able to handle responsibilities. I had hobbies. I had a career that pushed me towards my goals. I even went to the gym!

When you begin to think about what drives you and what you want from life, it is crucial that you don't start to feel selfish. The new life you are envisioning isn't going to be all about you. There will still be plenty of time for your loved ones.

What happens over the years is that our role changes. Each change that comes can result in a little bit of your identity disappearing. There were three major life changes that I experienced. Moving country, leaving behind friends and family was a little bit like leaving behind who I was. Meeting my partner, as time goes on you make sacrifices, unknowingly, you grow together, but you also become a different person.

Finally, I had children. This was the best experience of my life. It was also the moment I kissed goodbye to 'me time'. For a certain period of time, you are Mom. Your only goal is to take care of your children. I regret nothing. I just reached a stage where I needed to start finding who I was again.

Let's start with your passions. If you woke up tomorrow and had absolutely no responsibilities, what would you do? My mind first went to cleaning- my house would sparkle! No! This is a responsibility. While in the car on the way to work, I decided that I would go horse riding, swimming, read a book and probably binge watch a TV series with a glass of wine, heck, even a bottle!

From here, I discovered that I was still passionate about horses, swimming and books. I decided that the TV is great, but I wouldn't class it as a passion.

I moved on to think about what was important to me. Yes,

the kids popped into my head and I had to force myself to think bigger. One of the first things I thought of was my health and the health of my family. We eat well, but it certainly could be better. My home matters to me. I am the sort of person who has a list of DIY projects that I like to do. Finally, my friends and family hold a great place in my heart. Being away from them obviously means I can't see them as often as I want, but on top of that, even with modern technology, I'm not even in touch with them as much as I would like.

The last big question, and maybe bigger than the previous two, what do I want from my life? I've moved past the stage of wanting a new car, a huge house and lots of money. I want to be comfortable. I want enough money in the bank for holidays and emergencies. I love my job, so I don't want to change anything there, however, it would be nice to try something else. And I want my own horse.

Obviously, your list is likely to be completely different. There is nothing wrong with wanting to be the CEO of a multi-million dollar company. Your goal might be to have 10 children or to spend life traveling the world. Some people want to try bungee jumping; others may have a dream of buying their first home.

Your passion and what drives you might seem trivial to others, but that is irrelevant. This is the moment to think about you. At some point, your children will be all grown up and ready to leave the nest, you might be experiencing this now. You can't allow yourself to fall into the trap of having no ambition when this moment comes about.

If you can't think of anything, there is no need to despair or rush. Sometimes these questions can be overwhelming. It is advisable to talk to friends and family for inspiration. If possible, ask people who knew you when you were younger. Old school friends might jump-start the thought process with things like "Remember when you were really into..."

Sometimes, our chores are also our passions. I love cooking. I don't love the dread of thinking of what to cook for dinner each night. However, one of the things I love is baking. So I added this to my passions, not just to make the odd cake, but also to learn how to properly decorate them.

At this stage, if you aren't sure about what you want to do, or what your passion is, you can keep it general. For example, "I want to start a new hobby". What we are aiming to achieve is better time management, so you have time for the things you want to do. You can determine what to do at that time at a later date.

To recap, discovering what matters to you, your goals, and your passions doesn't mean you are selfish or neglecting other areas of your life. It's the first step to taking back the control and re-educating yourself about who you are. There is nothing driving you, you will struggle to find the motivation to make the necessary changes.

How to Make Time for What Matters.

So you have decided on your goals, your passion and what matters to you. Now it is the moment to start introducing small moments of time to start achieving what you want.

John Schorling is the director of physician wellness programs at the University of Virginia School of Medicine. Being a physician is a particularly stressful job that involves long hours and can take its toll on a person's health.

John states "balance requires effort, planning, and tradeoffs". He goes on to say that if we want a change in our lives, we have to be proactive. The change we want, no matter how much we want it, is not going to miraculously happen.

I made the mistake of jumping straight into my new life. I signed up for a Zumba class twice a week for my health. I bought cookery books for cakes, determined I was about to be on the best Bake Off show. And I opened a separate bank account to start saving.

Within the first month, I had $10 in my new account; I had made it to my Zumba class three times and baked nothing. I felt disheartened, like I had let myself down. My life was still crazy.

I wasn't about to let this put me off. This only meant that I needed to try a different strategy. This time I set myself a target for one week. In that one week, I wanted to find 10 minutes for myself, three times. In those 10 minutes, I was off the grid to everyone. I didn't do anything exciting, I read my book.

What this did teach me was that it is possible to achieve my goals if I started small. During that week, my family all survived, and nothing bad happened in my 10-minute sessions. It was time for me to get back on track with my goals. But I also learned that it's ok to readjust your objectives.

Remembering what John had said, I thought about the fact that money wasn't going to just appear in my account. So in my next 10 minutes, I made a quick financial plan to see exactly how much I could save and how long it would take me to reach enough for my holiday.

At this stage, the gym wasn't going to work. So I bought Zumba for the Wii and used the gym money for my savings account. Two birds one stone. I then took my ten minutes a day and used them for Zumba. It wasn't a lot, but it was a start that I could work on.

By now, you have probably heard enough about me and may still be wondering how this can apply to you. The concept is simple. Start small and be determined. Some of the things you want will be bigger than others. But all of them are going to take time.

If this is already something you are struggling with, you can't just say, I'm going to take three hours a week just for me. The chances are this will backfire, especially when considering your other responsibilities.

Exercise should be one of your priorities. It's amazing how just 10 minutes, three times a week started to help with other areas of my life. I was sleeping better, my mind was more focused and I had more energy throughout the day.

The Healthy Lifestyle Research Center at Arizona University carried out studies on the effects of short bursts of exercise, also known as fractionized exercise. The studies showed that three sets of 10-minute workouts could be more advantageous than one 30-minute workout.

The irony is, I had to get up earlier in order to do this. You may have to do the same if there is no other way to fit in some form of physical exercise. Remember, it can be anything, a walk around the block, look for yoga videos online, walk up and down your stairs for 10 minutes. You will soon notice your general mood lifting.

There are even a number of ways that you can incorporate fractionized exercise into your daily chores.

Leave your washing or ironing basket on the floor. Each time you bend down for an item of clothing, turn it into a stretch.

• Leave a set of weights in your office. While on conference calls you can be doing some bicep curls or squats for strength training.

• Don't sit at the kid's sports matches, walk up and down.

• Dance! I do this all the time (when nobody is watching). Choose 3 songs and dance to your heart's content while your cleaning.

Once you realize that you can achieve your smaller goals, you will start to feel more motivated about the larger ones. You can start to extend your ten minutes to fifteen. But my advice is to start with exercise.

Declutter Life!

In this section, we are going to cover the clutter we collect in our homes, workplaces, and minds. We will look at the physical and emotional effect of clutter, and some ways we can start to clear our lives from clutter.

Some people are blessed with the ability to have a perfectly clean and organized home. Others have all good intentions, but little people get in the way. There are a few people who pay no attention to clutter, not understanding the negative impact it can have on life.

What can also happen is that our clutter follows us. Our vehicles end up with extra shoes, last weeks jumper is still on the backseat. Does anyone else have a month's worth of mail shoved in the door pocket?

Then you reach your workplace. It's impossible to find anything as each paper gets put on the to-do pile rather than filed. You have tried to be organized with post-its, but now half are all over the floor, and the others make your computer screen look like a colorful bomb has hit it.

My worst clutter is that in my mind. It drains me. It's not just a case of the things I have to do. It extends to all areas of my life. The arguments I have had, the bills that I'm not sure if I am going to be able to pay, whether my work is good enough, whether I am a good enough mom.

I once watched a video by Mark Gungor. It was his guide to "laugh your way to a better marriage". Generally, I tend to stay away from men vs. women speeches as I feel that it doesn't promote equality. Nevertheless, Mark compared a women's brain to a huge bundle of electrical cables where each was connected to the other.

I thought this was such a great way to describe that feeling you get when your brain is so full, you don't know where to start. I kept trying to think of how I could just cut one cable. It might make the electricity just stop for a while so that my brain could rest.

Clutter in the brain will also have a massive impact on our health. Most significantly, I found that I couldn't sleep. I would wake up and remain awake for hours. Instead of sheep, all I could count were issues, things to do, and problems with my family.

If anybody else has experienced this, you will know that you won't be able to function during the day if you haven't slept. You will make mistakes that can cost you greatly, in the worse case scenarios, your mistakes could cost others.

Where do you start? This is going to require some family assistance because for a thorough declutter you are going to need a few hours alone. Explain to your partner, your mom or dad, even a friend that you want to make some change in your life, and you need to start with your home. Ask them to take the kids for a few hours.

There are no excuses here! If you aren't in the right frame of mind, choose a different moment. At the same time, don't keep putting it off; you will feel kilos lighter once the job is done.

Choose your favorite music, put it on nice and loud. Grab your big black trash bags and start upstairs. My general rule is "10 things have to go". So ten things from my wardrobe, 10 from hubby's wardrobe, and 10 from each of the kid's wardrobes. 10 toys, 10 things from the kitchen cupboard, 10 things from the living room, etc.

This sounds really brutal, I know, which is why you have to have the right mentality for this task. We get stuck in the mind frame of "Oh, but I might need that", or " I can't throw my kid's toys out". The reason you first went for that object is because your subconscious is already telling you that you don't need it.

I feel amazing after doing this. My home looks so much tidier, and it feels like there is more space. In terms of time management, you are making life easier because there is less to clean.

Make sure you donate all of the things to charity. This way, not only are you decluttering your home, but you are also helping out those who are in need, making you feel even better about your self.

You may wonder why it's best to do this task alone. First of all, the distractions will make this job take twice as long. Secondly, if your children see you throwing things out, they are going to get upset. If they never see you take it away, the chances are they will never know it's missing. I can say the same about my partner's things!!

Now it is time to declutter the mind. If you have never kept a journal, or don't feel that you would benefit, it's time to adjust your thinking. A journal is a perfect solution for emptying your brain of everything that is whizzing through the bundle of cables.

Have you ever started a conversation with your partner about how you feel but then completely lose your thought process? All of your words come out as if you were speaking Chinese, and your partner looks at you like you are mad?

Using a journal to write down your feelings is a method used to organize your thoughts. It's space for you to talk about the good and the bad in your life. It's your chance to vent without anybody listening.

While there is a myth about journals that it is just a book to keep all of your secrets in. This isn't true. Yet to some extent it should be treated this way. If you think that someone is going to read your journal, you won't be entirely honest about your feelings.

Remember, if you want to clear your mind from clutter, you need to get it all out, not just what you don't mind other people reading. Imagine an extended cable running from your brain, through your arm, and into the pen. All of the charge pulsating through your brain needs an outlet. Let this outlet be your pen.

For those of you who still aren't convinced of the advantages of keeping a journal, positivepsychology.com published a fantastic article about the benefits of writing down your feelings and emotion.

A number of psychologists and women's health experts contributed and listed some of the positive impacts your journal can have:

• It's a way of calming yourself and clearing your mind

• You have the chance to release bottled up feelings and stress

• You can let go of negative thoughts

• You can investigate your experiences with stress

• A journal can be used to write about struggles and successes

• You can learn about your triggers and become more self-aware

The key to keeping a journal is honesty. When I feel down or start to feel the stress of life come over me again, I look back at my life two months ago, or even six months ago. It's a wonderful chance to see how far I have come and how much I have grown as a person.

Make the Invisible Visible — Let's See What Needs to Be Done.

At this stage, you know what you are passionate about, you know what you want from life, you have started taking small moments a week to dedicate to yourself, and the positive effects of this should be starting to appear. You have decluttered your home, and your brain isn't so chaotic thanks to your journal.

But the work is not over. Let's begin to focus on time management during our day. Maximizing every minute you have, not just for work, but also for your family and yourself.

You may not like what I am about to say, but bear with me! I know that you wake up tired. I know that your body tells that that every minute in bed is necessary. We have to change this as soon as possible. Trust me, keep reading!

The first hour of the morning in my home is bliss. I am alone. My children are sleeping, hubby is at work, and there is absolute silence. It's a blessing. I do my Zumba, I shower, and I have my morning tea. Because I am alone, I get to appreciate a hot cup of tea, again a blessing.

While drinking my tea, I take my pen and paper, and I begin to write my to-do list for the day. Once I have finished, I stick it to the fridge. One of the major benefits of having this alone time is that you get to start the day fresh. I can't wait for my kids to wake up. In the past, I would wake up and think, "Here we go again".

To-do lists can be your worst enemy or your best friend. You probably think I am dramatic, but you have to know how to write them and use them to work in your favor. This will lead to negative outcomes if you scribble down a few things and assume they will get done.

Your to-do list is another method for decluttering the brain. All the tasks you need to get done that day should be written down. I find it necessary to do this in silence because I hate adding things to the list during the day unless it's urgent.

Keep your handwriting neat; a scruffy list leads to a scruffy day. Plus, it's annoying when you can't work out what you wrote at 7 am.

Some people like to have their list in order. The biggest jobs first or the most important. Personally, I write things down as they pop into my head. If I am feeling little down, stupid things like when the weather is bad, and I am not as motivated, I make sure I put a few things on the list that are super easy.

So now your mind is decluttered, and you can clearly see what you need to achieve for that day. It's a case of working through things and ticking them off. Now, I have debated this with my dad a lot. Do you tick or cross it off? He ticks, he likes to keep it tidy. I cross it off as I get more satisfaction, I can almost aggressively say, done! If you are a tad OCD, you may want to cross out things with a ruler, whatever makes you feel good!

Whether you tick or cross is a personal choice. What is incredibly important is that you are the person removing the task from your list. This to-do list provides *you* with a sense of achievement, that *you* are making progress. It defeats the purpose when someone else ticks off what *you* have done.

Finally, try to find some reward for completing your list. It could be something trivial like a bar of chocolate or an extra 5 minutes of alone time. Reward yourself for your success.

Shrinking the To-Do List.

As I said before, to-do lists can be an excellent way of decluttering your mind and organizing your day, but they have to be used in the right way. Here are my common mistakes when I first began writing to-to lists:

• Over planning, too many things on the list

• Unrealistic planning, not thinking about the time for each task

• Not balancing the tasks on the list

• Not allowing room for the unexpected

The first issue is obvious. You wake up feeling all determined, and you write 100 things to do. Granted, they all need doing, but it's just not possible to do it all in one day.

The second problem comes when you write down ten things; it's a manageable amount. But let's say I wanted to write 5 articles for my blog, invoice 4 clients, do the ironing, go shopping, pay the electric bill online, take kids to the dentist. I haven't included the usual things like take kids to school, feed animals, etc.

Each blog post takes at least an hour to write, as does the invoices, the ironing, the shopping and the dentist-if we are lucky. You have 9 things on your list that will take up at least 9 hours. Now if you have added absolutely everything on the list, the dishes, vacuum, walk the dog, cook dinner, be 'taxi' for kids, swimming practice, you can soon see that you do not have enough hours to achieve everything.

Balancing the tasks is something I learned early on. Every day we will have things that we don't want to do, it's a horrible fact of life, but they still have to go on the list. You cannot possibly have a list full of horrible things. Your day will drag on, and there is no fun. Life is too short for days like that. Here is one of my lists from last week:

• Zumba (love)

• Ironing (hate)

- Clean out the fire (hate)

- Make steak and Guinness pie for dinner (love)

- Write 3 chapters of my book (love)

- Decent walk for the dog (don't mind)

- Tidy kids clothes (don't mind)

- Plan and teach 4 lessons (hate the planning, love the teaching)

- Fix wobbly table leg (love)

- Gas in the car, mechanic for new light (a necessary evil)

- X1 washing (don't mind)

You can see that my list had a balance of good and bad. Some of my tasks were 5-minute jobs, others a bit longer, but overall, the list is balanced.

There will be some days when something happens that will set you back from your tasks. This will often lead to frustration as you feel you won't be able to achieve everything. This is why it is necessary not to put too many things on the list. Give yourself some room in case there is an incident out of your control.

I really struggled keeping up with my lists when I had my second child. Having a baby requires a lot of flexibility, and you can't always do the things you need to. I strongly recommend having a daily list and a weekly list.

Keep your daily list practical and doable, especially until you settle into a routine. If you have written your list and begin to feel overwhelmed, it's because there are too many things to do, and it's time to shrink it.

Nowadays, I keep daily and weekly lists (I did say I was a bit of a fan of the to-do lists). When I prepare my list in the morning, I revise it. If there are non-urgent things, they get moved to the weekly list. By doing so, I have taken the pressure off myself, however, I still have enough to give myself a feeling of achievement.

The things that are on your weekly list will still get done. What you will find is that by succeeding with your daily to-do lists, you will feel more motivated and energized to complete some of the weekly tasks.

Now that we have removed the physical and mental clutter and the responsibilities are clearly written down, it's time to learn how not to add to your perfectly organized day. There is one tiny little word that you are going to learn how to say in chapter 2 in order to improve your time management.

CHAPTER 2. THE MAGIC OF NO

Have you ever noticed how it's so easy to say no to your children, yet almost impossible to say no to adults? We wonder why our toddlers continuously say no when it's logical when we say it so often to them.

Most people are inclined to want to help. Perhaps the school is having a cake sale, and the teacher asks you if you can bring something. It's impossible to say no, so you find yourself making 100 cupcakes at 11 pm.

Your boss has asked to bring forward your deadline in order to keep the clients happy. "Absolutely", you say. Or maybe you are your own boss, and your client needs your undivided attention on a Saturday morning. Anything to keep the client happy!

Every time you say yes, another part of your life is going to suffer. If you are making 100 cupcakes at 11 pm, you are going to be tired and irritable the next day, possibly unable to carry out your tasks. By agreeing to work commitments, you will either be taking time away from your family or from your free time.

Sometimes we say yes without thinking through the logistics of a situation. We can't see our own mini butterfly effect that we are about to set in motion.

Let's take working on a Saturday. Originally you had planned to clean the house, do the shopping and take the children to their sports event. The house will have to remain a mess, and this will frustrate you. Your partner will have to take the children, resulting in you missing out on what's important to them. The shopping can be done in the afternoon, but then you won't be able to go to the cinema as a family.

The one tiny word "yes" has ruined your weekend and probably upset your family. Even when we do think about the consequences of saying yes, we are still unable to say no.

It generally comes down to the fact that we like to please people. We are under the impression that is everybody else is happy, you are happy. You can think of nothing worse than attending your brother-in-law's dog's birthday party, nevertheless, you say yes to keep the peace at home.

Nobody wants to be known as the negative person in the office who always says no. So we say yes. This problem has a tendency to grow. If we become a person who always says yes, people begin to ask us for things just because they are going to hear the answer they want.

Learning How To Say No.

So as not to come off as rude or abrupt, saying no requires a certain amount of skill and an awful lot of practice. It also requires a mindset that cannot be wavered. When first learning to say no, if you don't sound confident, the person may find a way to appeal to your better nature and get you to say yes.

Don't waste a no if you feel like you are going to say yes in the end. Some people will see this as a sign of weakness and use this to manipulate you.

When learning how to say no, it is best to start off with people you feel comfortable with. Avoid totally rejecting your boss's proposal without learning a few of the tricks first.

I found it best to start off with people who I am closer to, people who understand my personal situation more. My mom called once and asked me if she could come the following day for lunch with the other grandchildren. The idea was lovely, and I should have said yes. But it would have involved extra shopping, cleaning, missing my deadline for work plus half a day, which I had already filled up with other things.

It hurt me to say no. In fact, my mom was slightly taken

back. I did quite a poor job, really. There was that moment of awkwardness on the other end of the line, and we both hung up feeling a little shocked. It took me 10-minutes to phone her back and apologize. She said she would clean, do the cooking, I wouldn't even notice them there. We all know that wasn't going to happen, so I arranged a date for the following week when things could be organized more in advance. After explaining the situation and resolving the problem, we both hung up for the second time feeling relieved.

When you are put in a position when you feel the need to say no, focus on what words you use to accompany this powerful little word. No by itself is abrupt, almost rude. No with a lengthy explanation into all of your weekend plans is far more than your boss needs to here.

Keep your no short but to the point. Here are some examples, many of which are phrased in a way that doesn't even require a no, but the message is still clear:

• "I wish I could, but I already have plans."

• "I'm sorry, I can't. I have promised my family I will do something that day."

• "No, I'm afraid that's not possible."

• "Unfortunately, it's too short notice, and I am already busy."

Try to avoid clichés like "I will check my diary and get back to you", or "maybe next time". Phrases like this are just cover-ups and will leave the person feeling like they have been lied too.

How To Stand Up For Yourself and Still Win the Respect of Others.

When we use the word no, we need to try and use it in a way that doesn't create negativity. When I was talking to my mom, I shouldn't have just said no. Straightway, I should have explained why and put forward a suggestion.

This is true when dealing with work situations too. You are not going to get far in your career if you just say no all the time. You need to present a suitable alternative to resolve the problem you and your boss face.

Your boss has asked you to come into the office on Saturday morning to prepare reports for Monday's meeting. Imagine the three potential answers:

1. "No, Sorry I can't".

2. "No, sorry, I can't. My gran has an ingrown toenail, and I promised I would take her to the clinic she takes forever walking, and the traffic is going to horrendous…"

3. "No, sorry, I can't. I have committed myself to my children's football match. What I can do it take the work home and complete it in time for Monday".

You can see that the third option will show your boss that you are dedicated to your family and your promises, but at the same time, you are able to find a solution to resolve the problem. If your boss doesn't respect you for this type of response, personally I fell it becomes their problem, not yours.

Body language has a huge part to play when you are saying no. Shrugged shoulders and poor posture might suggest a lack of confidence, leading others to think they can convince you to say yes.

A lack of eye contact can suggest the same thing. It can also come over as slightly rude. Rude behavior, combined with the word no, is not going to encourage others to regard you in high esteem. Try not to keep your hands behind your back; it implies you are hiding something.

Most importantly, you need to smile and pay more attention to your micro-expressions. While you may feel stupid at first, it is always recommended to practice in the mirror so you can see exactly what the other person can see.

I have this habit of raising one eyebrow. Sometimes it goes so high it's like a puppeteer is pulling a string. It's my "as if/don't you dare look". If I smile as this wandering eyebrow starts to rise, I have noticed that I have an expression of fake content. If the eyebrow goes up alone, my boss might think I am acting like a hormonal teenager.

It is so important for me to get my message across clearly to control my micro-expressions. What your face says has to coincide with what your words are saying. Remember Dale

Carnegie's Poem about smiling "It costs nothing, but creates much".

Stand up tall. Be proud of being an assertive person. If your answer is polite, understandable and offers some kind of solution, there is no need for you to feel nervous or embarrassed. Standing up for yourself doesn't make you a bully or selfish. It shows that you are conscious of all of your responsibilities.

Learning how to say no in the right way will lead to many positive outcomes. Your clients and/or boss will develop a new level of respect for you. They will see you as a person who knows how to manage their time properly, as someone who is a problem solver and not as someone who can't handle their workload.

Finally, learning how to say no is an action that will make you feel proud of yourself. I could work every minute that I am awake. But when I say no to a deadline because I want to watch a film with my kids, I no longer feel guilty because I am not working. I feel proud that I am spending precious time with my loved ones.

Let's end this chapter with a quick recap of the steps we have taken so far:

• We have rethought our passions, life goals, and what is important to us.

• We have started taking small sessions of time to dedicate to ourselves, slowly increasing this time as we see fit

• We have changed our morning routine, allowing for a bit of peace and time to focus on the day ahead

• We have started some form of exercise to concentrate on our physical well being in order to improve our mental well being

• We have decluttered our minds and our homes

• We have learned how to prepare to-do lists to maximize your time and gain a sense of achievement

• We have learned the power of saying no and the positive outcomes it can have

Hopefully, at this stage, you can see small improvements. Don't forget that we are trying to make a drastic life change so it will take time. You may have fallen off the wagon (so to speak) and need to go back a step. This is not bad. Every small effort you are making now will have amazing results.

If you feel that you have mastered these steps, it's time for us to move on to the next step to improve our time management, and for this, we will focus on our homes.

CHAPTER 3. CREATING RELIABLE HOME AND WORKING ROUTINES

Simplifying System and Routines.

When I think about home routines, I think about my younger years when it was just me. I ate when I was hungry, and I went out when I felt like it. If I didn't fancy going shopping, there was bound to be some 2-minute noodles in the cupboard. Routines were only for work; the usual get up, go to the office, keep my head down and finish at five.

Some people aren't at a stage in their lives when they really need a routine. If you are reading this book, you desperately do, or the routine you have isn't working. There are cases when a routine has become so strict that it has a negative impact on family life. Let's cover this first.

It's a common occurrence for new moms to become slightly obsessed with routines. It's not our fault. We hear it drilled into us "routines are good for babies", or "everything will settle down when you get into a routine". But we set up our routine, and life doesn't seem to slot into what we had expected it to, or worse.

I'm not saying these words of wisdom aren't true. But some moms begin to fear the routine. They can't go out because baby is sleeping or it's a bad time to meet friends because baby has to eat. I have heard of extreme cases where moms just don't leave the house.

If we aren't careful, we can let our life be ruled by the routine when, in fact, we determine the routine. It is a tool to assist us.

The first step to simplifying our routine is to identify each aspect of the day, and I like to determine whether they are fixed or flexible. Let's take the day of a self-employed mom of two and separate her daily responsibilities.

7 am-8.30 am - the pre-school routine. Kids up and ready, shower, coffee. Check emails. Quick clean before leaving up. Leaves house at 8.30 to take kids to school.

9 am-1 pm - in her office, just her and her administrator. They divide up the day's tasks and start.

1 pm - quick lunch at her desk.

1.15 pm-5 pm - client meetings, conference calls, clean the office for the next day, invoices, and update budgets.

5pm- 6.30pm - kids have swimming practice/ homework club/ etc. There is an afterschool activity each day.

7pm- 9pm - evening routine. Dinner, homework, showers, attempt to be a good mom and spend some quality time with kids.

9 pm- bedtime - check kid's agendas, finish off last minute jobs, a quick tidy up.

You may think I have just made this up, but rest assured, this is actually my sister's daily routine. The first thing you will notice is that there is absolutely no time for her. Which is the first thing that has to change?

Some parts of our daily routine are more difficult to change. Our working hours are often fixed, so rather than stressing about how we are going to change this, look at the areas that are flexible. Morning routines, evening routines and the routine we have within our working hours can be adapted so that our lives run more smoothly.

When going over her routine, there are some things that could be simplified. The pre-school routine is something that can make or break a person's day. It is essential to get this right in order to start the day as you mean to go on. There is no room for error.

Is there really a need to check emails as soon as you get up? Our predecessors never had mobile phones with emails, and they were very successful and running companies. Our smartphones have taken the 9-5 concept and turned our working day into 24 hours.

Dedicate the mornings to children. Check the agendas, talk to them about what will happen in their day. Take an active interest in their lives. You will feel like a better person for doing so. Even if it's just 10 minutes, try and sit down and have breakfast with them.

If you don't have children, it's still no excuse to start going through your phone. Use this time to get in a little bit of exercise, even if it's just 10 minutes like we mentioned before.

If your children are older, get them involved with the cleaning up. As a team effort, it will take you less time, and it will also teach them that it's everybody's responsibility, not just yours. There will be more on this topic later.

When looking at the morning routine, keep it as simple as possible. I'm a fool because there are many mornings when I'm carrying baby, rubbish, and bags to the car. It's a disaster waiting to happen, and it flusters me. The rubbish can be done at a different time. The bags could be put in the car before the kids are up. These all sound like little things, but they will make a difference.

Everybody's work routine is going to be different, and quite often, a lot of the events will be fixed. In order for us to enjoy our jobs, it is important to have a routine that allows for everything to get done, but at the same time, some flexibility so that we can shake things up a little.

Here are some ideas that could make your work routine a pleasure rather than a pain:

• Walk into your office with a smile on your face. Be a happy person. After taking the kids to school, have a karaoke session in the car.

• The mornings are when we are at our best. Try to schedule the more challenging tasks for when you are more motivated and energetic.

• Buy a hotplate for the office. You will be amazed at some of the lunches you will be able to make. Take turns with colleges to make lunch. Make an effort to eat together, whether it's for one hour or 30 minutes.

• Alternate tasks based on the time they will take. If you have one long task, do a few short ones in between so you feel like you are making progress.

• Similarly, alternate tasks you enjoy and don't enjoy.

• Take regular, short breaks. Step away from your desk to change the scenery and, if possible, leave your mobile behind.

There are two points that require further discussion. First of all, the mobile phone. Don't get me wrong, they are fantastic and in many ways have simplified our lives. At the same time, we have become addicted to the beeping and the ringing. I know so many people who become distracted by their phones because they are constantly with them.

It's not necessary, nor is it healthy. And don't use the excuse "but what if there is an emergency". All I am suggesting is that for 5 to 10 minutes, you leave the phone on your desk. The idea of a break is to disconnect, and you can't do that if you are still reading client messages or emails from your boss.

Secondly, the lunch breaks. Many moms will notice that they have very little time for a social life. The lunch break is a great way to talk to colleges about adult things. Avoid work topics. Get to know the people in your office for who they are, not what they do. 'Jill from accounting' is more than just Jill from accounting!

The evening routine is a tricky one. We are once again torn between doing what our children want and doing what we need to do. I confess, there are some after school activities I will go to and take my laptop. It's a necessary hour that I can use to get ahead, prepare the next day, or finish off a few jobs. However, I have explained to my children the situation and made sure they understand.

Don't use this time for important work jobs. You will be easily distracted. Also, if there is an official event like a competition, don't work. Your children need to see your support.

The evening routine becomes more flexible again. To keep things simple, try to do your jobs while the children are busy with theirs. This will free up time for you to spend together without your mind being distracted.

Some parents need to sit down with their children to help with homework. This is usually a nightmare of a task. Use a timer. Explain the exercise, double-check they understand. Tell them you will be back in 10 minutes to check and help them with the next stage. This allows you to help your child, but at the same time, you have room to get a few other things done.

Creating a Routine That Works for You.

With an infinite number of work commitments and family routines, it is impossible to declare one routine as the best. Everybody's personal situation will have an effect on the routine. Perhaps you are pregnant and trying to figure out your new routine, and maybe you have an amazing partner who takes care of the children- then again; maybe you are a single mom.

By listening to how other people handle their routines, you may find inspiration, but be wary of trying to copy it. Somebody else's routine is unlikely to suit your situation.

Whether people know it or not, there is already an element of routine in our lives. What you need to do is to adapt this to make sure you are getting the most out of your day.

Then we have our weekly routine. While not every day is the same, most weeks are. Here are some of the elements of my weekly routine:

• Monday: Planning for the week

• Tuesday: Work out of home- not in all day

• Wednesday: Lighter day used to finish off jobs

• Thursday: School activities, late home, dinner already prepared

• Friday: Work out of home all morning, don't finish till 7.30 pm, no work after

• Saturday: Shopping

• Sunday: Cleaning/Washing

My routine works for me. Not everybody can handle the stress of shopping on a Saturday and may prefer to do it on a Friday after work. Some are lucky to have a cleaner and don't need to dedicate Sundays to the home.

While these activities are completed each week, it's also important to realize that nobody is going to die if something doesn't happen. I can't beat myself up if I choose not to work on a Saturday and go out for the afternoon. That being said, I have to appreciate that on Sunday or Monday, I will have more work to do.

At work, it may not be possible for you to change the order

of the day to get the most difficult tasks done first. In that case, it's important for you to use your morning wisely to achieve as much as possible so that the afternoon is saved for the challenging work. It is also even more important that you take a good lunch break, eat healthily, and stretch your legs.

Working from home does have its disadvantages, but I try to use it to my advantage. When establishing my routine, I tried to make sure that all the jobs that required my full attention were planned for the times I am alone.

This doesn't necessarily have to be work. If I have a blog article I need to write, and the topic is quite light, I know I can do it when the kids are around. So instead of doing that while they are at school, I will do the ironing (ironing with a baby takes twice as long).

Here are some things that I would recommend fitting into your daily routine. I find that they are quite necessary in order to have a positive and fulfilling day:

• A 15-minute clean up: Kids toys away, tabletops cleared, kitchen wiped down, floors vacuumed.

• 10 minutes of exercise: It improves my overall health, and even when I'm tired, I feel more energized.

• 10 minutes just for me: This is not selfish. This gives me time to compose myself, plan the day, and drink a hot coffee.

• Time for the family: 30 minutes minimum for family dinner, at least with the children.

• 2 hours of hardcore work: A set amount of tasks that must be completed.

The following things I try to include in my weekly routine:

• 45 minutes to watch my favorite series

• One activity that the kids want to do

• Two hours of heavy-duty cleaning

• Family exercise session, walk in the countryside

Again, these things work for me, so don't feel that you need to implement the same routine. I choose to get up earlier for my exercise and time alone; you may have a gym class that you attend. You might prefer reading a book to a TV series. Nevertheless, I do suggest that this 45-minute treat is uninterrupted.

As I have said once or twice. We have become too dependent on our phones, and it is a good idea to try and have some time away from technology. Although there are some people, who like to use apps to help them manage their lives. This is down to your preferences.

According to producthunt.com, here are some of the best apps that can help you plan your routines:

Taskade: Track daily tasks and routines from your Chrome or Firefox browser

Chaos Control: For personal project management and entrepreneurs with cloud integration

Streaks: A to-do list app that helps you stay on track of your daily routines

Habitify 3.0: iOS habit tracker that provides data analysis

Play around with some of these apps. Choose one that you feel comfortable with. At the same time, don't let it occupy too much of your day. If it's complicated to set up or run, uninstall it and choose another.

Please don't feel that an app is going to change your life. They aren't necessary, but they are tools that can help some people, just as a pen and paper will help others.

Creating or Changing Habits of a Lifetime.

How many times have you woken up on the 1st of January and decided it's time to diet, and you will go to the gym three times a week? How many times has this failed? Do you think you would have more success if you decided to add two more pieces of fruit or veg to your daily meals and exercise for 10 minutes a day?

It's the same with your routine. It is impossible for people in our situation to wake up one day and expect a change. There are too many other people involved with our routine that this will affect.

Imagine if a CEO woke up and said: "Sorry, I only have

conference calls from 10 am to 11 am". I think about what my partner would do if I turned around and said: "From now on, Tuesdays and Thursdays you have to take the kids to tennis, cook dinner, feed them, bath them and get them to bed, Oh, and don't forget the homework, cleaning, and dog!"

By expecting a sudden and drastic change, you are setting yourself up for failure. And if you want your new and improved routine to last, you are going to have to make the changes bit by bit.

More often then not, the habits you have, or the routine you are used to is something that is embedded into you over a number of years. While it isn't going to take years for you to adapt to a new routine, it is going to take time.

The first thing you need to do is to make a plan of how to get from A (your current situation) to B (the routine you would like). Make a note of the changes that will affect your day and make a separate note of the changes that will affect your family. Write down some ideas on how this can be achieved.

Next, you need to explain to your family that you want to and need to make some changes. It is important here that you discuss the changes as a family. Don't tell people that this is what is going to happen in order for you to improve your routine.

The idea that needs flow throughout the conversation is that the changes are good for everybody and that if everybody can cooperate, there will be more time for the activities that the family enjoys.

Go through your ideas. Ask your family for their options and if they think it is possible. Most importantly, ask for their ideas. It's amazing what things little people come up with that adults don't always think about.

Include your partner's ideas. Initially, I forgot this. Then I realized that if he was contributing, he would be less likely to work against the new routine and more likely to work towards it.

Once the whole family is on board, you can start making small changes. My favorite small change was trash. Instead of me making numerous trips with the recycling and trash, the kids agreed that this was a job they could do. I was really pleased about this because I felt this was a great way to get them to appreciate the environment and do their part. It was also a task that didn't require great change, but it was one less thing for me.

We also converted Friday into pizza and movie night. The condition was that everyone had to make sure that their bits and pieces were put away at the end of each day, and as a reward, we would treat ourselves on Friday. This required absolutely no work for me on a Friday night, which tied in nicely with my work routine.

In terms of work routines, I worked on a similar theory.

Most people have heard of the "work husband/wife" term. It's that one person you completely relate to in the office and work well with. If they are in the same department as you even better, if not, you can still use them as a sounding board, and there could be ways to work together.

During a lunch break, brainstorm with your work husband/wife ways that you could adjust the working routine in order to maximize the day. There might be some tasks that you could take in turns to do so that you are saving time, for example, trips to other departments or photocopying.

One thing I like to do is my 10-minute leg stretch with a colleague. It gives you both a chance to disconnect. Plus, if you commit to a short walk with someone else, you are more likely to get away from your desk.

If your schedule allows for it, you could set the same "hard-core" work hours. If you and your colleague both have a list of 5 things to do in 2 hours, you might find a bit of healthy competition motivates you both.

When you are creating these changes, try to set yourself some deadlines. Again, this will depend on how drastic your changes are and/or how many changes there are. Divide your plan into various days or even weeks. Each week add a few changes to your routine.

There is no quick fix. The key is taking control of your routine and making the decision to change. This can be done instantaneously. Coming up with a plan with your family or coworker may take an hour. But if you want the changes to last, you need to take the process step by step.

Don't worry if everything doesn't work out exactly as you planned. We are human, after all, and you have to allow for mistakes. Whether it's you or someone else involved in your new routine, let them know it's ok. A small setback is not a sign of a failed plan. It's important to put it behind you and stay focused on achieving the other changes.

You also need to bear in mind that there are things in life that are out of our control. People get sick, cars break down, and school holidays are one of the most frequent causes of an upturned routine.

All of these things we must take in our stride. Our routine may have to be temporarily adjusted. This is why I always advise people to have a routine, stick to it, but it's not written in blood!

If, for any reason, you need to change your new routine because of outside influences, remember what is important to you and the new routine you created. If you find your 10 minutes of alone time in the morning has had a significant impact on your life, make sure you include it in your temporary routine. The same applies to things that have become important to your children.

To sum up routines, they are an incredibly helpful behavior that will help you to maximize your day and keep those around you happy. Routines should be suited to the individual and flexible to an extent. On the other hand, don't let your routine become so flexible that you don't respect it.

Hopefully by now, you will be feeling more positive about your daily and weekly routines. The work isn't over. Our next aim is to maximize the things we can achieve with the time we have available.

CHAPTER 4. BOOSTING YOUR PRODUCTIVITY

Time Management.

This is important and can make or break a day, a business deal, how people view you as a person, and even your relationship. Your time management relates to your level of respect for commitments, and it defines your reliability. Ultimately, your time management is going to play a huge role in your success and how you feel about yourself.

While being a serious section of this book, I don't want to terrify you. So I am going to tell you about one of the most frustrating things about my relationship. Feel free to laugh.

As you have probably guessed by now, I use every minute of my day. It's all planned, every task, every break, and every commitment. My partner, on the other hand, is a complete free spirit and will never be ruled by time. Ironically, he is the first person to complain that he doesn't have enough.

So, one day he tells me he is going to do the cleaning. I am thrilled and take my computer to start working. First, he has to smoke, and this takes 10 minutes. Then he checks his phone, by now I am twitching. Then he has to choose the right music and so on. It takes all my effort not to just do it myself. His whole "warm-up to cleaning process" takes the same amount of time as it does for me to clean.

My partner has no concept of time management, and this leads him to being angry and often complains at his lack of time. In turn, this makes me angry because I can't get through to him that he needs to be wiser with his time.

Some reading this will agree with me, others will like the idea of taking their time to do some tasks. There is certainly an argument for both sides. But we are here to get the most out of our time, and this means we have to reconsider the way we approach our jobs.

I'm not saying that I am like the road run and speed through my day without time to enjoy it. My approach is to do the work in the set time and then reward yourself. If you feel the need to catch up on social media, that's fine. But don't do this before you have completed your tasks.

Being good at time management is just like following a recipe. If you throw all the ingredients into a bowl and cook it, you might get a decent cake. If you follow the steps to make the cake, you will have a light, fluffy sponge.

If you have planed your day correctly, you will have included a timeframe for most of your tasks and responsibilities. Now it is a case of following the steps in your plan just as you would in a recipe.

Let's take a look at how you can include successful time management into your planned day.

You will have a rough idea of the time it takes to complete different tasks. I know that I can research and write a blog in around one hour. If the topic is more complicated, I allow for two hours. Monthly invoices will take an hour and a half. Shopping takes me 45 minutes. Walking the dog another 15 minutes, etc.

Make a list of your tasks and the approximate time each one takes. Be honest with yourself. If there are any tasks you are unsure of, write down an estimate and confirm it the next time you have to do it.

There is no sense in telling yourself a task will take one hour when it usually takes two. It's highly unlikely that you are going to achieve it in two hours. The only thing that will come about is that you will lose an hour of your planned day. This will have a knock-on effect on the other things you need to do.

Over the next couple of days, pay close attention to how much time it takes you to do things. Right now, it's not about doing the jobs faster. It's about managing the time you have to achieve the things you need to do.

Energy Management.

It's all very well writing to-do lists and creating a new routine, but if you don't have the energy to carry out your responsibilities, you will be back to square one. You begin to feel frustrated, drained, but too exhausted to do anything about it.

You have already heard me enthusiastically talk about starting the day with 10 minutes of exercise. I had to wake up earlier to fit this into my routine. I felt the day began with more positivity and more energy. I felt better about myself, and I began to feel more confident.

Remember, this is not a goal to lose weight. If you want to lose weight, you will need a completely different set of goals. In this section, we are going to look at ways you can manage your energy levels to be able to carry out your daily tasks.

There is scientific evidence to back my happiness and increased energy. Pete McCall is an exercise physiologist. He says that the reason we start to feel more energetic is because of the increased blood flow when we exercise. More blood flow around our body means that our muscles and organs are receiving more oxygen. He further explains that by increasing cardiovascular activity, your body is better able to produce energy in the form of a chemical known as adenosine triphosphate.

Here are some other benefits of exercise:

• Improved circulation

• More control over blood sugar

• Burning calories

• A release of endorphins

• Mental clarity and improved memory

The National Sleep Foundation goes into detail about the studies carried out to demonstrate increased exercise with improved sleep patterns. After 4-24 weeks of regular exercise. People with insomnia fell asleep more quickly and slept for longer. It also helped reduce signs of anxiety and depression. There may be a correlation between exercise and reduced insomnia because of the effects on the body clock.

Now that the scientists have explained why exercise is good, let's recap in laymen's terms. Exercise can increase the blood flow around the body, helping to deliver oxygen to muscles and organs. It can prevent various diseases. It releases happy hormones, and it can help you sleep.

It's not just about exercise. Your diet has a massive effect on your energy levels. I really struggled here. It's not that I'm a chocoholic or have a bad diet. I'm just very fussy and don't like a lot of food.

There is no need to go on a diet to increase your energy levels. It's about making sure you eat enough of the right food. Here are some foods you can try to introduce to increase your energy levels:

• Bananas

• Fatty fish (tuna, salmon)

• Brown rice

• Sweet potatoes

• Eggs

• Apples

• Quinoa

• Yogurt

• Seeds

• Beans

• Nuts

• Green tea

I started a very simple rule that helped me increase my energy levels. Whenever I had a craving for something sweet, I had to have it with a piece of fruit. This way I wasn't denying myself my treat, but making it a little healthier.

I also replaced my first cup of tea with green tea. Sometimes I drink hot water with a slice of lemon. People swear by this for a boost of vitamins and cleansing the body.

Introduce your energy management plan slowly. There is no sense in signing up for the gym if you don't have time. Start off small but make a start. Get the kids involved with planning new meals. I give my daughter two new ingredients and ask her to find a recipe for us to try.

Productivity Tips.

We have already covered dome ideas for you to be productive, but we will quickly go over some of the key concepts again:

• Create to-do lists wisely, understand the necessary time for each task

• Try to stay away from social media sites, or if you must, check them in your breaks

• Avoid multi-tasking

• Develop a routine that suits you

So let's look at a few other tips.

Understand your 'Time-Wasters'

There are some things, habits I have that I know waste my time. That being said, I used to find it difficult to stay away from them. Pottering is one example. I would walk around the garden, pick up this or that, pull out a weed, Google how to take care of something. In my head, I was doing something constructive, but really I was just wasting time.

There are so many distractions online, which is why I keep advising you to stay away from the phone. Whatever your time-wasting demons are, write them down so that you are fully aware of them.

Take advantage of dead time

Traffic!! Oh, it drives me mad! I feel like it's such a waste of time. Moments like waiting to pick the kids up or waiting for appointments. Each moment may only be a few minutes, but this is a time that could be put to good use.

When possible, use the time to send a few emails or reply to messages. Pay the bill that is on your to-do list. If you can't, focus on mental planning. I use dead time to revise my goals, see if there is anything new I want to achieve or even mentally calculate my budget to see if I am on track.

Know when perfection isn't necessary

Everyone wants to do their best, but is it always in your best interest. Cleaning your home is the best example. Nobody wants to live in a dirty mess, however, if I wanted my house to be as clean as I would really like, I would be there all day.

If you need to produce a report for a team meeting, your PowerPoint presentation has to be great, but not every image has to learn up perfectly, not each font has to be identical. Save your perfectionism for client meetings.

Stop waffling

Have you ever had to listen to your boss go on and on when

the main point of the meeting has over 20 minutes before-hand? Have you ever sent an email that was far longer than it needed to be? A lot of the time, we waffle, adding fillers where no filler needs to be. Take all of this out and save yourself some time.

If you are running the meeting, say what needs to be said and then wrap it up, your colleges will also appreciate this. Save those long family chats for when you know you have the spare time.

Get to know your keyboard

Your keyboard has a surprising number of shortcuts that will increase your productivity while working. Learn how to use keyboard shortcuts. At the same time, consider using a password manager. This can save a lot of time trying to remember each considering the average person has 27 online passwords.

80:20 rule

Also known as the Pareto Principle is a fascinating rule derived by Vilfredo Federico Damaso Pareto. The rule states that 80% of the results will come from 20% of the action.

The theory behind it is that by doing less, you will achieve more, however, it certainly doesn't mean being lazy. It's about choosing your time wisely.

I have always been somewhat skeptical about theories and principles, and before I invest my time, I like to know that these things work. So here are some fascinating 80/20 examples I found.

• Pareto discovered the rule when he noticed that 20% of the pea pods he grew produced 80% of his annual peas.

• He continued to explain that in 1896, 80% of the land in Italy was owned by 20% of the population

• Today, 20% of the world's richest people have 80% of the world's income.

• Microsoft reported in 2002, 80% of errors were caused by 20% of the bugs involved

• 20% of customer complaints come from 80& of the clients

• Even 20% of your clothes are worn 80% of the time.

So how does this help us? 20% of your actions will lead to 80% of your results. When you look at your to-do list, you will see that some activities are part of the bigger picture, your long-term goal. Others have less meaning. Hanging the washing out isn't going to get me closer to earning money for my holiday.

You need to focus 20% of your actions each day towards those tasks that are going to bring you closer to your goal. These tasks must be done when you are at your most productive. I call it "I'm on fire mode". Save the other tasks for another part of your day.

To implement this rule correctly, you first have to learn

when you are most productive. There is no right or wrong answer here. Some people prefer the mornings, others the evenings. There are people who have more energy after lunch, and I often hit a bit of a wall.

Once you understand when your peak times are, you will be able to look at your to-do list and structure your day more accordingly.

Focus.

Sometimes I envy our ancestors. I am convinced they had fewer distractions in their time. I can't blame friends and family for sending photos or funny videos (and neither can you, by the way) because it's my choice to pick up the phone. I will even go as far as blaming my baby because she makes me laugh so much!

There are moments when we are distracted; there are other moments when we simply can't muster up the ability to focus. Let's cover what to do in each situation.

You have been working for 30 minutes, you are on a roll, but all of a sudden you start to slow down. There are distractions that are causing you to lose focus. You must fix these right away. If not, you are going to waste time.

If the TV is on, turn it off. If you keep singing along to songs on the radio, turn it off. Maybe the noise from outside is disrupting you, and you work better with background noise, turn the radio on. If you have pets that are pleading for your attention, put them in another room.

If your phone is beeping, check to see what the issues are. If it is nothing important, put your phone on silent. If there are messages that need dealing with, either add it to your list for later or if it's quick, handle it in the moment.

If your family members need you, deal with them. I upset myself when I say, "Give me 5 minutes" because I know I need more than 5 minutes. You aren't solving anything, just delaying the inevitable, in 5 minutes you will be interrupted again.

So what happens when there are no distractions, but you still can't focus? If you are stuck in a moment like this, it's time to change the strategy and do something else. I know that on my list, I have many other things that I could be doing rather than hoping that I will become focused.

Walk away from the task. Have a coffee if you feel the need. Continue with some other shorter jobs so that you still feel like you are making progress. While you are doing your other tasks, mentally prepare for what you need to focus on. If you are having a quick clean up, visualize the plan for your next task.

When you feel more mentally prepared, begin the task that requires your focus.

Multi-Task Less, Achieve More.

I was talking to a male friend of mine one day, and he made an excellent point about why men tend to be better chefs. I huffed and puffed but decided to listen. He said that when men cook, their complete attention is dedicated to cooking. When a woman cooks, she often has to entertain the kids, get lunches ready, tidy up, and really a whole possibility of jobs.

I wish I had time to stand over the stove for an hour each night, lovingly stirring my food and adding in a pinch of this and that. Of course, my food would be better. But the reality of it is that I have a number of other things that I should be doing. In fact, I would feel guilty, as if I was wasting time.

Multi-tasking is a great ability to have in certain situations, however, in others, it doesn't do us any favors. Typically for me, the result is a burnt saucepan.

And it doesn't stop there. Multi-tasking and work can lead to mistakes. If an accountant is switching between paying employees and preparing invoices, the various figures are going to start getting mixed up. Nobody wants to see VAT charged on their payslip!

Some jobs require multi-tasking, in particular when working with children. I marvel at how my daughter's nursery teacher is able to juggle six babies at the same time. Nevertheless, when her teacher goes home, there is still little benefit to multi-tasking.

Multi-tasking is like an adjustable showerhead. You can choose between a larger flow of water with less pressure, or you can concentrate the flow so that you receive more pressure.

When trying to achieve several jobs at the same time, you are dividing your skills and assets. Each task gets a little bit less of your attention. As a parent, I can't possibly pay full attention to my work if I am trying to help my kids with their homework. Now each task only gets 50% of me. If I'm trying to do three things, this is reduced to 33%, and so on.

Not only does a task receive less attention, but it also ends up taking longer. Writing 500 words should be a 20-minute task. If I have to keep stopping to listen to my partner, this becomes at least 30 minutes. Add on the extra 5 to 10 minutes to revise my work, and the task has now doubled in time.

Doesn't it make more sense to focus all of your efforts on one thing before moving on to the next? You will save time and complete the task to a higher standard.

This is also advantageous when working with to-do lists. If you have set yourself a goal to complete three tasks in an hour, for example, you will feel more motivated ticking on task off when it is finished quicker than ticking three off after more effort.

Don't get swayed by peer pressure. You may overhear someone saying how quickly they can get things done because they are so lucky they can do more than one thing at once. Anybody can do more than one thing at the same time, it doesn't mean that things are done well.

Tricks for Getting More Done.

Time management is so crucial nowadays that we are lucky to be able to take advantage of a number of tried and tested methods. Here are some of my favorite tricks that will allow you to get more done:

Make Your Bed and Keep Your Desk Clear.

These are two habits that people use on a daily basis. Making the bed for me is necessary; I can't stand getting into an unmade bed at the end of the day. It's the first completed task of the day, which gets you on a positive start.

Keeping your desk clear allows you to keep your mind clear and have sufficient space to work. Others argue that a messy desk is a sign of intelligence and creativity. Maybe, but it going to distract you from the tasks at hand.

Get Enough Sun.

No, it's not time to go and sit on a beach. It's time to increase the amount of natural light you receive. Sunlight is full of vitamin D and a wonderful natural energy booster. Make sure you drink plenty of water too.

Do It the Mediterranean Style.

It's funny; I have spent the whole book telling you to maximize the use of your time. But, there comes a point when you are just so tired you are not at all effective. Make a short nap; some say 10 minutes, others 30 minutes. Set an alarm, so you don't snooze away the afternoon. A 15-minute nap will completely recharge your batteries without making you feel groggy. You will then be able to carry on being productive.

Listen and Teach Your Children to Listen.

When you actively listen, you take in all the information, and there is less room for mistakes. It will also save you time having to listen to the conversation again. Teach your children the same habit. If necessary, tell them to repeat what you said. It will save you time having to repeat yourself.

The Two-Minute Rule.

The two-minute rule, by David Allen, simply states that if a task takes two minutes do it now. This is a great way of crossing off some of those little important jobs and making you feel like you are making progress.

The Pomodoro Technique.

We have already covered the concept of breaking down your working day into blocks. Personally, I can handle two hours.

If you feel like this is too much, try the Pomodoro Technique where you work for 25 minutes and then take a 5-minute break. Be sure to use a timer so that you stay on track.

Learn How to Be Better.

Education is a real motivator. If you are unsure about something, or you feel that you could do it better, research how. This may involve a short online course or just a quick Internet search. Learning new skills will lead you to feel more confident.

Read This Book.

It's an obvious one, really, but so many people will read a self-help book and not follow the advice or even blame the book for things not working out. I read many books and took a little advice from each. You might read these tips and think they are awesome ideas. If you don' put the ideas into practice, they are just that. An idea rather than a solution!

Delegate It.

In the home and the workplace, we tend to develop this sense of having to do everything ourselves. You can't ask your administrator to do it because they already have too much on their plate. You might feel it's not fair to ask the kids because they need time to relax. Your partner has also had a long day, so it's probably best for you to do it. Change this mentality right away.

We are going to cover the home more in more detail a little further on in the book, but for your own sanity, please remember that you all live together under one roof. It's everybody's responsibility to take part in chores, and more importantly, there own space and things.

Your partner has probably had a hard day, but then so have you, and your day has far from finished. By asking family members to take care of a couple of jobs, it will free you up both physically and mentally in order to be able to finish other, more important jobs.

Delegating at work isn't just about making your load a little lighter. It gives your team or employees the chance to demonstrate their skills, take on new responsibilities, and progress in their careers. When you delegate tasks, you are showing people that you trust and respect them.

Jenny Blake is a career and business strategist, and she suggests you first need to decide on which tasks can be delegated. If you have a task that falls into one of the 'Ts', you could delegate it:

• **Tiny -** lots of little jobs that take up your time

• **Tedious -** tasks that don't require your skills and can easily be done by someone else

• **Time-consuming -** break one large task into smaller ones and delegate small tasks to others

• **Teachable -** educate your staff, teach them how to do things so that you don't have to

• **Terrible at -** Admit it, some staff have more skills than you do. You might have a social media wizz kid who can update your company profile better and faster than you can.

Once you have decided that a task can be delegated, you now need to choose the most suitable person for the job. This person will need the right set of instructions to carry it out. I find it helps to explain why you have chosen them for the task. In this manner, they feel special rather than having to do a task because you can't be bothered.

Whether you are delegating at home or at work, remember to check the job has been down and provide praise and feedback. A thank you will go a long way for the next time you need to delegate.

There are a huge number of things that you can begin to implement in order to help increase your productivity. Some things like exercise and improving your diet will not just allow you to achieve more, but they will also allow you to feel better about yourself. You will become happier and more confident.

Due to the number of tips and tricks in this session, it is even more important not to try and begin them all at once. You will overwhelm yourself, and while trying to keep on top of all of your new systems, you are likely to become less productive. Always bear in mind that slow changes will lead to long-lasting changes.

Finally, don't forget that everyone is different, and much of the advice can be adapted to your personal needs. Start off by choosing some of the things on this list that excite you and motivate you. If there is something that you feel doesn't work for your situation, change it. I exercise in the morning;

you might find that evenings are better for you. Most importantly, make sure the changes you make lead to a more enjoyable, productive life.

At this stage you are probably feeling all jazzed about your motivation and productivity, and this is brilliant. Let' remember that it isn't your job to do everything. Some simple cooperation from family members is going to free up a significant amount of your time.

CHAPTER 5. FAMILY COOPERATION

Creating a Home System with Clear Roles and Clear Expectations.

One of the main reasons women and moms become so weighed down is because of the number of roles we take on. First of all, there might be your professional role. Nowadays, it's often not enough to fulfill one role in your job, so you may have to juggle multiple roles within your career.

If you are self-employed and/or working from home, your professional roles may extend into an accountant, cleaner, administrator, human resources, etc.

When you get home, you are then challenged by another set of roles; mom, cleaner, cook, taxi driver, nurse, teacher, personal shopper, etc. It's normal with such a wide range of responsibilities to feel overwhelmed and unable to get through everything you have to do in one day.

The problem is, now that we have these roles, it's almost impossible to change them. Your children won't understand if the next time they get a cut, daddy has to make it all better. You can't simply refuse to cook one day, or not wash their uniforms.

What you can do is ensure that the family members are each playing their part in the running of the home. Imagine from now on you are running your home like you would your own business, you are the manager, let's say your partner is the team manager, and the kids are the staff. Rather than you being in charge of everything, you have your responsibilities and you oversea everybody else.

While dedicating roles to family members, I would keep such titles to yourself. Hubby might not appreciate being your second in command. And you don't want the kids telling schoolteachers that they are working for "mommy"! Rather you being in charge of everything, you have your responsibilities and you oversea everybody else.

When I wanted my family to cooperate more, I decided I needed to think about what chores were appropriate for the age of my children. I even printed off a chart for my older daughter, and the results were amazing.

Not only did she take on the jobs in her age group, but she also began doing jobs in the next age group up to demonstrate how grown up she was. So you can see what I'm talking about, take a look at some of the age-appropriate chores:

Ages 2-3

• Pick up their own toys and books

• Wipe a table clean

• Put dirty laundry in the basket

• Do the dusting (help with the spray)

Ages 4-6

• Feeding the pets

• Lay the table and help to clear it

• Help fold the laundry

• Put away grocery shopping

• Make their own bed

• Tidy their room

• Take out some trash

Ages 7-10

• Sweeping/vacuuming floors

• Collecting mail

• Water plants

- Help wash the car

- Put the washing machine on

- Help with preparing meals

Ages 11+

- Wash the dishes or load the dishwasher

- Mop the floors

- Clean the bathroom

- Clean out the fridge

- Begin with simple recipes

- Help with younger siblings

- Clean windows

I found that being aware of what my children should be able to do helped me to organize the household chores fairly. It was also only fair that they completed their homework and had time to rest first.

The same way that we changed our routine slowly, you need to encourage family cooperation in the same way. It's a little harsh for you 4-year-old to wake up one day and have 5 extra daily jobs.

Start off by adding on small tasks, for example, a 3-year old can help you with the dusting once a week and tidy up their own toys every day. You may have to help them in the beginning.

When you are asking your children to take on new responsibilities in the home, you have to teach them first. What might be second nature to you won't be to them. They won't know how to clean a bathroom, or how to load the dishwasher safely. This is certainly important when your children are beginning with food prep, where hygiene and safety are necessary.

When asking for your partner's cooperation can be heaven or hell, depending on your man! I have found that partners can be completely understanding and take on their fair share. There are others that need some training, but we make an effort. Then there are some that can't seem to see things from your point of view and you end up having arguments.

The first and second are great. You can communicate, you share the household chores, and although they may not always do things the way you like them, the jobs get done.

I find it hard with the third type of partner, and unfortunately, this is such a stereotype that I face. I even resorted to writing down all the tasks I did and those that he did. But he was unable to see that the balance of household chores was unfair.

This is really hard and can be heartbreaking. You loathe

being the woman that nags all the time, but you can't find the solution. There are two options:

1. Accept that this is your partner, and things aren't going to change

2. Put your foot down and show him that this is not the way your family home is going to be run.

I might sound like a really horrible person here, but I refused to do his washing or ironing. If he left his shoes in the living room, he would have to hunt for them in the garden. I stopped buying his favorite foods.

He had to go shopping. He had to wash his clothes by hand because he still didn't know how the washing machine worked. In the end, he realized that putting the washing machine on was a lot quicker than hand washing.

Whether you choose option 1, 2, or continue to try talking to your partner is something only you can decide on. Every couple is different. My choice was extreme, but with a full-time job and a new baby, I was desperate, and our relationship was heading towards the end.

Before going down either root, you need to make sure you have made every effort to have a sensible, levelheaded conversation without arguing. If you can afford to, it is well worth hiring somebody who can come and clean once a week, even if it's just for a couple of hours. It will free up your time and prevent arguments.

If you can successfully teach your children that the home is everybody's responsibility, regardless of age or gender, you will be setting the foundations for when they have their own families.

Treat It Like a Game and Have Fun.

Ok, so that was the heavy side of family cooperation. Now let's work out how we can make running the home a game rather than a chore.

When my daughter was younger, she saw me preparing the staff contracts, and I had to explain what a contract was. This led me to the idea of a contract for her. After weeks of nagging her about her room, I blitzed it and took photos. I added these photos to our contract.

Our contract included the following:

• I am your mom, not your slave

• I will help you as much as I can but only when you make an effort

• Your job is to study and keep your room tidy

• If these two jobs aren't carried out, there will be consequences

• If your bedroom is not the same as in these photos, I will take your phone away

• If the room continues to be in a state, there will be no after school dancing, and I have the right to come in with a black bag and throw out everything you leave on the floor.

Singing a contract really worked for us. She was able to read everything that she was agreeing to. After the first time, I did the black bag trick she was devastated but soon learned that a contract is a commitment that must be stuck to. Don't worry, I gave her back the black bag after she had learned her lesson, I'm not that cruel.

Setting up contracts with children might not sound like fun, but it is a guaranteed way of reducing how much you have to nag them to get things done. In the long run, your life will be easier without having to be the grumpy mom.

Just like you want to have some fun while working through the chores, so do the rest of your family. In fact, if you are in the right frame of mind, doing the chores can be quite enjoyable, especially when you get to see the results. If your family sees you having fun, they are much more likely to enjoy themselves too.

The family having fun and starting a water fight while washing the car doesn't have to only happen on TV. If it's a bright sunny day, have fun outside. It might take you longer than planned, but the car will be cleaned, even the patio will be washed down, and you will be spending quality time with the family.

Make sure there are rewards for everyone at the end of your chores or when a child learns how to complete a new task alone. Rewards can be something small, like a bag of sweets or their favorite cake. Or it could be something bigger that they have been working towards for a while, like a trip to an amusement park.

The rewards that you set have to correspond with the size of the task. They should also be individual. My partner doesn't get excited over pizza and a box of chocolates, my daughter does.

Sometimes, it is nice for the whole family to work towards a common goal. I do this is we can keep things up for a long time. For example, 10 days without anything left on the floor and we will go to the zoo. Have a wish jar where you can each put in ideas for rewards and things you want to do.

Some Gamification Ideas.

First of all, you might need to adjust the ideas depending on the age of the children but here are some tried and tested ideas that not only work for me, but for lots of other families I have spoken to:

Hide the treats: Before setting everyone off to tidy up their rooms or even just the toys, hide a few things to surprise them throughout. Younger children will enjoy finding stickers or sweets under their toys. I slip in a few coins for older children, for example, when they are making their bed or putting away their clothes.

Basketball laundry: Take the laundry basket to the child's room and see if they can aim their clothes in the basket. If you want to extend the game, see who can get the socks in the washing machine.

Make a treasure hunt of chores. After each chore, leave a clue for the next one. At the end of their chores, make sure there is some reward to be found.

Beat the clock: This is often more motivating for older children. If they can do their chores before a certain time limit, they are rewarded. I usually say things like, "clean the bathroom in 15 minutes, and you have 30 minutes of video games".

Competition time: Take the weekly cleaning chores and divide them into the age-appropriate groups. See who can complete their list of tasks first. The winner gets to choose the family activity.

Chore Darts: Instead of having a regular dartboard, stick chores on the board. The kids will try really hard to hit the chores that they want to do.

Chore Board Games: You can download printable board games that are designed for the family to complete chores. It's not a speedy way of cleaning, but it is a great idea for raining days. If you can't find one that is suitable, make your own.

Use Star Charts: Probably one of the most common methods to motivate younger children is to use start charts. Each time they complete their task, they can get a star, once they have collected enough stars, they are rewarded. While the concept is designed for older children, if the prize is right, I have seen this method work just as well for older children and teenagers.

Try not to get frustrated, particularly with teenagers. It's impossible for them to realize that we were once that age, and it's impossible for us to work out what is going through their minds. Rather than getting any when things don't go your way, see if they need help. We want the family's cooperation in order for the home to run more smoothly, but not at the cost of more arguments.

One last note! If you are working from home, this does not mean that you have more available time to do the chores. Try to make sure that all of the family members are aware of this.

Many times I have heard "but you have more time at home". This doesn't mean I have had more time for household chores. Reiterate that it's a family home, and it's the family's responsibility.

Have you ever noticed how much time you spend in your kitchen? If only there were some ways we could make meal preparation quicker without sacrificing our health. This is exactly what we are going to do in the next chapter.

CHAPTER 6. KITCHEN AND MEAL PREP HACKING IDEAS

There is no doubt that meal times occupy a lot of our time. Regardless of who is cooking and cleaning up afterward, a major part of our day is spent preparing meals. And it's not just the three main meals; many of us have to prepare snacks for children or meals to take to school and work.

Any parent will know that the fun really begins when you have fussy eaters, and it becomes impossible to prepare just one meal.

When it comes to dinner, in particular, there seems to be a whole lot of other jobs that start creeping up. Perhaps it's because we have all been out of the home for the day, or you haven't seen your family until now. I also find that people are normally more exhausted, and it's easier for tempers to flare. Raise your hand if you have been cooking, and your child passes a school paper to sign, and that was the final straw to make you snap?

It all sounds rather dramatic; after all, it's only cooking. I actually love cooking, but there comes a point when I feel the pressure of other tasks building up, and all I want t do is sit down with my kids and watch Peppa Pig.

While we can't eliminate this responsibility, we can certainly implement ideas that can save time and improve our health as well as make the process more fun. The first section of this chapter may involve some shopping, so get out your credit card and don't feel guilty!

Tools and Equipment to Have Handy in Your Kitchen

A slow cooker

When I gave birth to my second daughter, my mom bought me the best present ever! Others filled my home with much-appreciated clothes and creams, whereas my mom bought me a slow cooker. I am not exaggerating here; my slow cooker changed my life.

In the morning, I am already in the kitchen with breakfasts and school snacks, so it's no great effort to throw some ingredients in the slow cooker and turn it on. During the day, the food is cooking deliciously. All you need to do is serve it when you come home.

Here are some amazing ideas for your slow cooker:

- Slow-cooked beef and broccoli

- Chicken Tikka Masala

- Casserole

- Fish stew

- Any type of curry

- Whole roasts

Really, there is no end to recipes you can make in a slow cooker. The great thing is that they don't cost a fortune either. You can pick one up now from $50 to $100. If you can, it's worth investing in one that has a large enough capacity for your family.

Also, look for one that comes with a warranty, and there are even some that come with recipe books.

A vegetable slicer

For as little as $10-$15 you can pick up a vegetable slicer with a range of blades to cut, chop, slice and grate fruit and vegetables. Not only will this save you time, but it will also encourage you to eat healthier.

I use mine to make quick snacks for the kids, sliced apples and pears, carrot sticks, and cheese cubes. Many come with safety features that will allow older children to use them too, although I always keep an eye on my oldest daughter when she is using it.

A knife sharpener

You will be amazed at how much faster you can cut food up with a sharp knife. Instead of trying to hack through your beef or chicken breasts, you can run your knife through a blade sharpener, and the knife will glide through food.

An all-in-one blender

Mine isn't too large, so it's not a hassle using it, but I can blend in seconds with a good quality blender. It makes great sauces, whisks eggs and cake batter, and best of all, baby food. My youngest eats the same as I do but just blended. It saves a lot of time in having to prepare an extra meal for baby.

Being able to make cake mixtures, cookie dough, and brownies in 10 minutes allows my children to have some sweet treats, but they are far better than shop-bought treats.

Non-stick all the way

Anything you buy from now on should be non-stick, utensils, saucepans, frying pans, baking trays, roasting dishes, you name it. There is nothing worse than looking at a load of pots and pans that you know are going to need soaking and scrubbing.

Even the dishwasher won't get some stains off. And leaving things to soak means your kitchen is never tidy. Some people prefer non-stick coated pans, others stainless steel, it's up to you. But if you look after them well, they can last for years, if not a lifetime.

When shopping around, you will find lots of cheap options, and there is nothing wrong with this. Amazon basics have a great range of things for the kitchen. Try to make sure whatever you buy is BPA free, so you aren't potentially affecting your health.

To Use the Dishwasher or Not to Use the Dishwasher.

Some people swear by it, others find it causes more arguments because nobody can agree on how to load it properly. Personally, I have never owned one. In fact, I rented a house once and used the dishwasher for extra storage!

If you are going to use a dishwasher, make sure that the whole family knows how to load it in a way that everyone agrees on. I think that loading the dishwasher is an easy job that everybody should take part in. If a toddler can pick up a tablet and load a program, they can most certainly put their own plastic plate in the dishwasher, the same goes for teenagers.

Never overload a dishwasher. It's the same as with a washing machine. If you put too much in, it won't clean everything properly. If you need to wash a couple of dishes by hand, you will save yourself time later on. Choose the best time of day to run the dishwasher. And again, everybody can take part in unloading it- not just you!

Finding Inspiration.

Half of my battle is that sometimes I don't know what to cook aside from the same old meals we always have. There are loads of ideas online, but I have found it is always best to have one cookery book that you can completely rely on for those days when you want to try something new.

My go-to book is called The Cooking Book, published by DK. There are loads of everyday recipes, recipes for dinner parties, desserts, baking, sandwiches, and soups, ideas for leftovers, even ways to spruce up your potatoes. There are a vegetarian section and techniques on how to carve, use pastry and make sauces and jams.

The great thing about this is that everything I have tried has turned out perfectly. The DVD really helped me to learn new tricks. I found one I knew how to joint a chicken correctly. I saved time and money. It also comes with a mini shopping list book to take to the supermarket with you.

On a similar note, I find that it really helps to have a well-stocked pantry. I'm not just talking about staple foods like flour, pasta, and rice. I mean the herbs and spices that you may only use once in a while. Powdered ginger is something that I now add to a lot of meals to spice things up, as I don't always have fresh ginger. The same goes for chili paste and soya sauce.

Have a Plan.

If I said I had a plan for every dinner, I might sound a bit rigid, or boring, that being said, having a plan keeps me organized and saves both time and money.

I prefer going to the supermarket once a week. During this trip, I make sure I buy enough food for 7 dinners and a range of lunch ideas. It's not to say that the plan is strict and one food must be eaten on a certain night, but I don't buy things because I fancy them.

Before you go shopping, think about the meals you want to eat this week. I try and keep everyone in the family happy while I am planning. Some ideas to consider:

• Chicken night

• Pasta night

• Fish night

• One throw it in the oven night

• Pork in the slow cooker night

• Vegetarian night

• Minced beef: homemade burgers, spaghetti Bolognese, lasagna, cottage pie

You don't need to know the exact recipe. There are endless things you can do with chicken. But if you buy chicken, you know you have it there for one dinner. The same goes for the other meats you buy.

Having a plan reduces wasted food, which I admit, drives

me a bit crazy. Nothing gets thrown out in our home. If it looks like some food is about to go out of date, I cook it up and freeze it, or look for a recipe that includes it.

While I don't like throwing out food, I am also not scared to make extra. Having leftovers is a brilliant way to have some extra meals saved in the freezer. I also love this idea for 'throw it in the oven night'. If I have leftover curry, spaghetti Bolognese and veggie stir-fry, we can cook up all of this quickly, and everyone can eat their favorite dinner.

Bulk Cooking.

Sometimes, it is well worth investing a couple of Sunday afternoon hours to cook a few meals. After all, once you are in the kitchen, it makes sense to take advantage of your time. You can make several meals in once and save them in Tupper pots or sealed bags.

Some recipes aren't as well suited to re-heating, so I would make them fresh that day. Others, for example, curries, taste better the next day. For this, you will need a good set of Tupper pots.

Some people prefer vacuum sealing food, which is again, is a great way of preserving food and saving money. As with the slow cooker, there are a variety of vacuum sealers available without costing you a fortune. Most even come with bags to get you going.

Between bulk cooking and the slow cooker, you can have enough meals without preparing a meal in the evenings.

Get Everybody Involved.

Some parents don't want their children cooking, as they are worried about the dangers. There are some things that older children can easily do, and I am of the opinion that there are other tasks that younger children can be shown. Remember, while it is your responsibility to feed your children, you are not the household slave.

From 10 years old and above, I think children should be able to boil an egg or put a pizza in the oven. They should easily be able to make sandwiches and weigh out ingredients to make a cake. Those children who are enthusiastic about cooking may even be able to make a simple pasta dish.

Younger children can butter bread, wash fruit and vegetables, and help you collect food from the fridge. Some may be able to cut fruit and vegetables, especially if you have children's safety knives.

Personally, I also think it is important for children to participate in cleaning up. They can wipe down the table and kitchen sides and even do the dishes. Make sure you wash anything shape and put it away first.

You may find that you have to re-do a bit of their cleaning up. Please don't get into the mindset of "it's quicker if I do it myself". Yes, this is true, but they are only learning. If they never get the chance, they won't be able to practice, and you will be stuck cleaning up forever.

Children of all ages can help with putting the shopping

away. Make it another game is necessary, but little ones can take the toilet roll to the bathroom, and older ones can stock up the fridge.

Equality in the Kitchen.

Last year I was teaching a class of 8-9-year-olds. We were learning about household chores and how the children can help out at home. One child said that her brother didn't have to do anything in the house because he was a boy. I was heartbroken and somewhat speechless.

It was unbelievable to think that we were still teaching this attitude. I quickly realized that if this was the attitude of the parents, this is exactly how the children will grow up. Looking at my partner that evening, it was clear to see that how he was bought up has a direct relationship with his participation.

Regardless of whether your partner does all of the cooking or none of the cooking, teach your sons as you would your daughter. Imagine what kind of a husband or partner you want him to be in the future.

Cooking is going to take up our time. Rather than seeing it as a chore, look at it as your source of energy and good health. As easy as it is to eat fast food every other night, this is going to have a seriously negative impact on your health. You will end up feeling unhealthy, bloated and lacking energy. With a good plan and a varied shopping list, there is no limit to what you can cook.

There is a whole world of cuisines. Sometimes all we need is a few new recipes to wake up our taste buds in order to find inspiration. Encourage your family to help. Ask them to look through the cookbook for meals they would like to try. Divide recipes up so that everyone can participate, and don't forget that everybody can participate in the clean up too.

If at all possible, invest in some of the kitchen tools I mentioned. If you can only afford one, make it the slow cooker. Add the other things to wish lists for birthday and Christmas.

While we want to eat as healthily as possible, everyone deserves a treat every now and then. Once in awhile, treat yourselves to a take out. Ban everyone from the kitchen so that nobody has to clean. This is a great way to reward yourself for staying on track with goals and to-do lists.

I have mentioned children a lot and for obvious reasons. Regardless of whether you are planning to have children, you are pregnant, or you already have a full house, the next chapter is dedicated to the little people in our lives that make time management somewhat more difficult, yet at the same time, make everything worthwhile.

CHAPTER 7. RAISING CHILDREN MADE SIMPLE

The hardest thing about my impossible schedule was (and sometimes still is) the guilt I feel for being a working mom. Even though I am now happy with my schedule and I feel like time management is no longer an issue, there are still moments where I wish I could give it all up and dedicate all to my girls.

We all know that in today's economy, this isn't possible. At the same time, I get frustrated because men (with the exception of stay at home dads) don't have to torment themselves with this choice. It's fine for them to go to work and spend a couple of hours with the kids in the evening. Why can women not take on the same attitude?

It boils down to society! Regardless of what is done to encourage equality, we are still living in an age where women are encouraged to go to work, yet frowned upon for leaving their children. We can't change society just yet, but we can change how we feel about ourselves.

To do this, I have always been quite honest with my daughter about my work and my earnings. For years after school, she had to come with me when I was teaching or when I had meetings. Our home during the weekend was flooded with students.

I took each class and explained how much money WE would earn. I explained that these classes would pay for the cable TV, these classes for our food, and then there were classes where we could enjoy the income.

Having my daughter understand the value of money and the necessity to work helped relieve me of some of my guilt.

Being a working mom means you are going to have to manage your time better than the president of the USA! There will be times when you are exhausted, pulling your hair out from the stress of your job, and all you want to do is disconnect. But you are going to have to bite the bullet and put your children's needs first.

It will be worth it, and you will enjoy spending quality time with your children. The question is, how do you balance the needs of your job with the needs of your children? There is no straight answer because we will have to consider the age of the children. So, let's break it down a little.

Understanding the Needs of Different Aged Children.

Pregnancy

Are you already sick of hearing, "A baby is going to completely change your life!" or "Make the most of it while you can, you won't be able to when baby comes". Let's get to the bottom of these words of wisdom. While I have to agree with both of them, these phrases are often used with a negative tone. I remember feeling terrified at the thought of becoming a mom because there would be no time for anything.

You are about to embark on the best experience of your life, and your perspectives will change greatly. Maybe you won't have the chance to go to the movies. As cheesy as this sounds, once a baby comes along, you might find more pleasure just watching them than anything you will see on a big screen.

Pregnancy and newborn babies are different for every single mom. My best advice is to do what you feel is best for you. While you are pregnant, try to implement some of the time management tips we have already mentioned. For example:

• Start your 10 minutes of exercise per day. Once you are in the habit, it will be easier to get back into it once a baby is born. It will also greatly help during labor.

• Prepare your kitchen with tools that will save you time like a slow cooker, a blender, etc.

• Eat right- it's a no brainer really. Your body needs additional nutrients and energy more than ever.

• Nap while you are pregnant, nap when a baby arrives. Every mom is tempted to clean and run around doing a million jobs when baby is sleeping. This is great if you feel you have the energy. If you don't sleep and never feel guilty about this.

• Begin to imagine how you would like your days to plan out with the little one. Babies need fresh air so think about the best time to go for your walks, when is the best time to do the shopping, cleaning, etc. Get used to doing these jobs with a baby. Sometimes it's great to rely on a family member, but you don't want to get in the habit of leaving baby with mom while you do the shopping or you will never be able to do it.

With my first daughter, I became slightly obsessed with reading online blogs and info. Be very careful of this. First of all, I read some blogs, and it just made me feel like I was doing a terrible job. Others came across with such urgency that I became too strict, and when things didn't go my way, I got more nervous. This was particularly true with feeding routines.

Take the advice you read with a pinch of salt. Try it, if it works for you brilliant if not, no worries. It doesn't mean you are doing anything wrong.

Finally, be wary of what you buy for your newborn baby.

We start reading about lists of everything we need. There are some things that you absolutely must have for safety reasons, such as a car seat. There are other things that honestly aren't necessary.

I found that my house became incredibly cluttered with things I either never used or used because they were there. The clutter actually drove me crazier than anything else. Get the basics. When baby comes, you will be able to have more of a feel for what you need.

Take time with your baby. Sit on a park bench, even if it's just for 5 minutes, listen to the birds. Appreciate that in this moment, you are the only people that matter to each other.

Toddlers and young children

I have a little inside chuckle at new moms who say that babies are hard. Babies are easy. You put them down, and they stay in that place! Toddlers are mobile, which opens your world up to a whole new set of problems. Toddlers demand a lot of attention.

It's a difficult time for your little one. They start to get an understanding of what they want, but they don't always have the ability to communicate this to you. This can lead to temper tantrums. Most parents have experienced this, and it feels like a never-ending moment with no solution.

Don't give in to the tantrum. Stand your ground. At this stage, your little one is testing you and your limits. The first few tantrums may be awful, but if you start to give in, they will learn that this is the best way to get what they want.

Trust me, this can take up a ridiculous amount of time. Suddenly, the 30-minute trip to the supermarket becomes an hour because your darling kid spends 20 minutes screaming on the floor because you have bought the wrong cereal. This is only amusing because you know it's true. In that moment, you wish the ground would swallow you up.

Setting limits and boundaries is crucial for little ones, and it will lead to much more enjoyable moments that you can spend with them. Everyone wants to take their children to the park, but it becomes a shame when the parent dreads going because they know there will be drama when you say it's time to leave.

Both toddlers and young children need stimulation. They need a wide variety of activities available to them in the home. In a perfect world, every activity will be educational and will focus on language skills, fine motor skills, problem-solving, and creativity. Sometimes, your children need to play with action figures or dolls.

I found that by having activities that I enjoyed, it was much easier to disconnect from work and the other responsibilities I had to do. One afternoon we made paper-mâché heads. The whole house was a disaster; we were both covered in sticky newspaper. But we had so much fun and at not one point did I think about work.

Organize your afternoons so that there is a range of things to do. Remember that young children have a short attention span, so avoid giving them all of the activities/toys at once. Divide the activities into things they need help with and things they don't. Here is an idea:

• Coloring/stickers/painting- this can be done at the same table where you are working. You are there for support, but you are also able to complete some little jobs that don't require great thought

• Toy time- your children can select their favorite toys to play with. Set a timer to encourage your children to make the most of their free time. You will be able to crack on with the household jobs or dedicate time to older children.

• Reading- stories and books are so important for children, and now is the time for children to develop a lifelong love for books. Read a story with them, help them read a book, talk about the book, what they liked and their favorite characters.

• TV time- Let's not be ignorant. At some point, children will want to watch the TV and in controlled circumstances, most think this is ok. Again, set the timer and make sure the program is suitable and where possible, educational.

• Homework- this is another activity that can be done at the table with you. Make sure you are there for any help or guidance, but don't end up doing it all for them. I like working at the same time as homework because younger children don't see it as a chore just for kids. It develops an attitude of "I'm doing homework like mommy".

Reason with your younger children. Be flexible to their needs, and don't get frustrated if you can't find the time to complete other tasks. Use phrases like "Ok, we can play for 30 minutes, and then I have to clean the bathroom". Don't just sit down and feebly play for a few minutes before disappearing again.

These are the years that you need to appreciate every time you hear the word "mom", even if it's 20 times in a row". It won't be long before your little one hits the preteen years, and you wish they would need you like before.

Preteens and teens

If you have reached this stage, you might feel like you have just been dumped! It's like it happened overnight. Or there is one instance where you know your child is growing up. I will never forget singing along to Gangster's Paradise in my car when this voice popped up from the back, "Mom, you're not 20 anymore".

I took this in my stride and decided to laugh, but it didn't stop me realizing that I was about to face a whole new set of challenges. Teenagers are scary, even when they are your own!

It's hard to understand what they are thinking. Their friends and their mobile are far more interesting than you are, and no matter how many times you say something, you are going to have to repeat it, a little bit like when they were five.

At this age, children are expecting us to treat them with a new level of maturity, but through no fault of their own, they aren't ready for it. On the other hand, some children want to be treated like adults but still have moments of acting like a child. While all of this is normal, it doesn't make it easier for you or them.

Despite your teenager thinking you are as old as dinosaurs, we do remember this period of our lives, and I certainly remember how difficult it was at times. I know and you know that juggling our responsibilities now is far more challenging than when you were 12 or 13, but teenagers haven't experienced this, so avoid telling them they have it easy. It won't help build an understanding relationship.

At the same time, the life of a teenager is nothing compared to "our time". There are far more dangers to be aware of, both on the street and online.

There will be a great swift in the dynamics of your relationship. It will go from them wanting all of your attention to you wanting their attention. Not in a needy way, but I still feel like a bad mom if I don't spend time with my teenage daughter.

Even if they don't want to spend time with you, you will need to make an extra effort to find things that you can do together. These moments are crucial for developing an open and trusting relationship.

There are going to be a number of topics that you cannot avoid when raising a teenager, for example:

• Sex- the good the bad the ugly

• Relationships

• Potential dangers in the world- knowing how to be safe without scaring them

• Drugs and alcohol- peer pressure

• Changes in their body

If you never spend any time with your teenager, how will they find the moment to talk to you about these issues?

Try not to sit down and have "the talk". It tends to put an element of awkwardness into the conversation. I find moments in the car are useful to start a conversation that allows my daughter to open up about something.

There were a few cases of drugs on the news, which I told her about. I told her about a video that we watched in school about a girl who died after trying ecstasy once. Rather than the usual "don't do drugs", I explained how the video terrified me into never taking drugs, even when my friends tried to encourage me.

You can't wrap them up in cotton wool and protect them from the world. You can only hope that your relationship is strong enough that they will come to you when problems or situations arise. This is much more likely if you spend time with them.

How to Build Strong Connections Even if You Have No Time.

Take a second to think about the relationships in your life with your parents, friends, co-workers, and your partner. Each relationship requires work and effort, and this is no different when you consider the relationship you have with your children. Just because you give birth to someone doesn't mean to say that your relationship is set for life.

It's a common belief by parents and bonding specialists that if a parent bonds with their baby, they are more likely to have a closer relationship with them in the future. So the first step to building a healthy relationship starts from day one.

Bonding with a baby doesn't have to come from the mother alone. Skin-to-skin contact is a perfect way for fathers to bond with their babies. Even newborns need to hear the voices, smell the scents, and feel the contact of mom and dad.

There are three things that I think are essential and mutual in our relationship with our children: Trust, Respect, and Honesty. These three elements should be considered in every step of a child's development. And the younger you begin, the better.

Your children have to be able to trust you. In a world that is so unpredictable, they need to know that they can come home to the safety of their mom (or dad) and know that everything is safe and as it should be. At the same time, for you to be able to allow your children more freedom, you have to know that you can trust them. Remind them that every action has a consequence.

The first time my daughter walked to the village shop, I followed her (haha, I know, a little extreme) but I had to make sure she was crossing the road safely, that she didn't talk to strangers, and most importantly that she went to the shop and came back.

When she got home, I confessed that I had been watching and that I was so proud of her. I told her that because of how well she had done, she had gained my trust, and I felt more confident to let her go out by herself more often.

Conversations with your children require patience and respect. They deserve their chance to speak just as much as you do. If you interrupt your child, you are teaching them that this behavior is ok. But then when they interrupt you, you tell them off. It's not mutually respectful. This is more relevant when it comes to teenagers, as conversations have a tendency to become more heated. Use a timer if you feel it is necessary. This way each person has the opportunity to talk while the other listens.

How great does it feel when your mom tells you that you are doing a wonderful job with your children! Your children need to hear your words of encouragement. They need to know that you support them and that you have confidence in their abilities. At times you will need to correct them, but you don't need to criticize them. Remind them what they did well and make suggestions on how to improve.

Then comes that stab in your heart when your child says, "Mom, I hate you". If you haven't had this yet, prepare yourself for it and remember that it's ok. Whatever insult your child throws at you, let it go. In these moments, they are so wrapped up in the emotions that they are feeling; they don't know how to express them. They are learning.

Take a very deep breath. Walk away for a few minutes if you have to but don't react. Let the tempers cool down before restarting the conversation. Explain that you are only human and have human feelings; words like that really hurt you. Discuss the root of the problem and find solutions together. Never brush a situation like this under the rug. It has to be addressed in order for it not to become a bigger issue further down the line.

Time Management for Raising Kids.

If you are reading this book, it is because you are about to embark on great changes in order to maximize your time. Don't get me wrong. When you get to the conclusion, you won't automatically have hours of free time to do all you want with your children. Building connections is going to require effort.

It is tempting to do everything your children want. Surely by doing this, you will be keeping them happy and happy children make for happy moms. Yes and no!

We already know that your time is limited. If all of your free time is dedicated to your children, you will leave no room for your partner or yourself. So it comes down to balance.

What many don't realize is that you don't need to spend every available minute with your children. They will come to rely on you too much and won't develop independence, a fundamental trait that everybody must learn. So, again, it comes back down to the balance.

During the week is the hardest time to dedicate to your children; however, raising kids includes preparing nutritious meals, homework, reading, hugs, playtime, bath time, etc. These tasks don't need to occupy more of your time, as they are already part of your daily routine.

When you are planning your time management, you need to ensure that at least some of these activities are dedicated only to your children. Leave work, computers, and mobiles for another time.

As I mentioned before, some activities can be combined with a few odd jobs so that your to-do list is shrinking. Homework and bill paying can be carried out simultaneously. Other activities like bath time and stories should be treated as your fun time with the kids.

For older children, you need to make sure they know you are

there if they want you or need you. I walk into my daughter's room, and I get the look as if to say, "What do you want". I know she isn't interested in spending time with me, so I will do other things so that I am free for her later.

Use some of your responsibilities to spend time with the children. Shopping is always a good start. Play supermarket sweep, give each child their own shopping list. Let them choose some meals. Although it's a household chore, it doesn't have to be boring.

Make the most of time in the car. Tell them about your day and ask about theirs. Don't ask out of habit, ask because you're interested. Play the best/worst part of the day game. You will be surprised how it opens the way for more conversations.

Raising children is the hardest thing we will ever do. We never know if we have got it right or whether we are permanently damaging our children. Do we spoil them, are we too strict? You feel bad for nagging them to eat their veggies, you feel bad when you let them eat pizza.

As much as we would love to be there all the time, it's not possible, and remind yourself that this is ok. Being busy doesn't mean that you are abandoning them, and it doesn't make you a bad mom.

Make the most of the daily responsibilities with your children. And really make the most of those times when they don't need you so that you are available for them when they do need you.

It's only far that after talking about our kids, we spend a little time working towards a better relationship with our partner. Yes, they drive us a little potty, but the next chapter will provide you with some tips on how to strengthen your bond.

CHAPTER 8. A STRONGER, BETTER, DEEPER RELATIONSHIP WITH YOUR PARTNER

As if you didn't have enough to juggle, now you have to consider spending some quality time with your partner. Unfortunately, as you are both adults, and there isn't as much responsibility as with work, your relationship with your husband/wife is often left till last or even completely abandoned.

When the kids are finally asleep, if you are anything like me, you will use this valuable time to finish of your to-do list rather than sitting down and talking to your partner, or even just enjoying a hug while watching TV.

A lack of time with your partner can lead to devastating consequences. It is also the sort of problem that creeps up on you without knowing. One minute everything is fine, then, slowly over time, you grow further apart. Before you know it, you are two different people with little in common.

Another frequent occurrence is bickering. Nit-picking at each other's bad habits until there is an explosion of emotions. I'm not going to go into the negative effects of arguing in front of children. It's patronizing, as we know that our children suffer.

At the same time, nobody is perfect, and I would be lying if I said we have never argued n front of the children. All I can say is that if it does happen, be honest with your children. Where possible, and appropriate, explain the outline of the problem and reassure them that it isn't their fault. Never blame the other parent. Your children need to know that you and your partner are an indestructible team.

While on the topic, it's also worth bearing in mind that arguing can be healthy. In fact, according to a study carried out by David Maxfield and Joseph Grenny, couples that engage in healthy conflict are ten times more likely to have a happy relationship.

Of course, healthy conflict doesn't involve insulting each other and then walking away, leaving the problem unre-solved. In order to deepen your relationship, you need to be able to air out the issues. I like to see it as a relationship spring clean.

Let's take a look at a situation of mine that many can relate to.

Þ We both come how from work, we are both tired, in fact normally I have to work for an extra couple of hours, however, his job is physical and mine is mental, so I try to appreciate this.

Þ He leaves his shoes in the hallway, unpacks his workbag, and all of a sudden the clean kitchen is a disaster.

Þ He overloads the washing machine yet doesn't put it on.

Þ I hear constant complaints that he is tired, never has time to himself, and never gets a chance to relax despite sitting on the sofa watching cartoons with our daughter.

I can cope with the shoes, I bite my tongue at the mess in the kitchen, I try to calmly explain that the washing machine won't work when it's too full (and unless you switch it on), but then the combination of these things along with the complaining causes me to snap.

I know it's wrong, I know it's counterproductive, but it happens. The result is that a cloud of negativity ruins our evening. If this behavior isn't discussed, it won't be corrected, and therefore, the same pattern will be repeated the next day.

These are examples of smaller, niggly issues, but the same thing will happen with larger issues if you don't communicate. Here are some tips on how to keep your conflicts healthy:

• Stay away from discussing things on the phone- you need face-to-face communication in order to be able to read your partner's body language as to communicate effectively

• Stay away from your bedroom- you may be tempted to discuss your problems in the bedroom away from the children, but your bedroom is a place for sleeping…and sex, don't make it a negative area.

• Stay focused- it's easy to start talking about the problem at hand, and then all of a sudden your complaining about your mother-in-law. Really, your mother-in-law isn't a problem, but you have strayed from the topic, looking for more fuel for the fight.

• Use a timer if necessary- similarly to with your children, arguments lead to interrupting, which is a massive sign of disrespect. If you feel this is happening, use a timer, so each person has the opportunity to speak.

• Listen- and not just with one ear open. Listen with your entire heart and mind. Think clearly about what the other person is saying. You are not a mind reader, so you can't assume you know how they are feeling. Put yourself in their shoes before responding.

• Watch your vocabulary- be careful of things like "It's so selfish when you come home from work late without telling me". Try things like, "It makes me feel like you aren't thinking about the family when you don't tell me your plans". You have eliminated the insult and explained how you feel.

• End on a high- yes, you are in a rush and have many other things to do, but take a minute or two for a hug and a kiss.

Physical contact releases those happy hormones we all need.

It's easy to find fault in your partner. It's not so easy to look inside yourself and see what you do to drive your partner a little crazy. What things can you do to reduce the tension in the air? I'm not talking about being a good housewife and making sure the house is clean, and the dinner is on the table. Sometimes just showing a little interest in their day is enough or buying their favorite dessert.

Find Time for Your Love.

It feels like the only solution to time management is by spending more time on things. Just like the relationship with your children, you and your partner need to spend time together. And, just like with your children, it doesn't have to be a lot, nor does it have to be every day.

Couples need time apart to be themselves, to practice their hobbies, or see their friends. You can't criticize your partner for wanting to go out for a beer.

"A robin redbreast in a cage

Puts all heaven in a rage"

William Blake

Being cooped up together all the time is not a sign of undying love. Spending time apart isn't a sign of problems. On the contrary, this will provide conversation topics other than just the working day.

Nevertheless, it will become a problem if your partner is constantly out, or if you don't have the same opportunity to spend time with your friends or your hobbies. Your relationship needs a healthy balance of space and time for each other.

But how is dedicating more of your time going to help with your time management? It's quite simple, really. When you are both happy in your relationship, you will first save time by not arguing, and you will find that your partner is more inclined to participate in the home.

It's actually amazing the difference it makes. When my partner and I are happy, we go from bickering over who is going to do the cleaning, to him actually saying he is going to do it. Which, in turn, makes me happier, and our relationship even stronger.

Again, it's a small example. But a lot of the time, if we work on solving the smaller issues as they occur, we are less likely to experience the bigger problems that are much more complex and difficult to fix.

When you think about spending time with your partner, it has to be productive time or active time. We may think that 10 minutes on the sofa sat next to each other is spending time together. It's really not.

Our time with our husband or wife needs to be the time when you focus on your love. You need to put the phones down, talk to each other, be physical, and laugh. You need to be able to talk about your feelings. This is your time to be you, not a mom, nor a boss, just you. Remember the people you were before children and work took over your lives.

Other times it might be a case of watching TV together or reading books and enjoying the silence. But you can do this with a cuddle or holding hands. As with your children, when you dedicate time to your partner, make it count.

How to Create Your Dream Relationship Even if You Have a Busy Day.

So, we can separate this into two areas of our lives. There is time for your loved one throughout the day, and then there is the bigger picture of time during a week or month. Let's look at how we can develop our idea relationship during our busy week.

I think, like most areas of time management, it's necessary to have a plan. After work, we still have our household chores, after school activities, and if we are lucky, time for ourselves. Logically, nothing is going to go right if everything happens in the same evening.

We have covered ideas for making dinnertime easier, so here is an example of a week that could allow everyone to do the things they want to do. Your week could be adapted depending on your schedule.

• Monday: after school activities, you take the kids, hubby has time alone at home

- Tuesday: work together on household responsibilities, time for your hobby

- Wednesday: after school activities, hubby takes kids, you have time at home alone

- Thursday: slow cooker night, nobody has to cook, there is time for both of you to have at least half an hour for yourselves and family time

- Friday: hubby has time for his hobby

It might come to a Friday night, and you have a night out with your friends so that you can switch a Tuesday to a Friday. You might have after school activities every night, so obviously, time will have to be divided differently. I try to have at least one night where we are all home. Even if it means your hobby time is at the weekend.

However, you divide the week up, make sure you sit down together to work on a plan. Try not to treat your partner like another child and make their plan for them. For it to work, and again, work long-term, you need to agree on the schedule, and it has to be fair.

During the week, you can use some of your responsibilities to spend time together. Cooking together is a lovely activity. It gets a job done, but at the same time, there are no phones to distract you from the conversation. If one person is doing the ironing, the other person could be in the same room playing with the children or helping with homework. Turn the TV off so that you are not all glued to it rather than talking.

Walk the dog together or do your 10-minute exercise together. We are not one of these fitness couples that perform yoga poses together, but doing sit-ups together is a real giggle.

Don't go to bed at the same time as the children. Sometimes it's all too tempting, and sometimes it's fine. But there has to be some time for just the two of you. Even if you are tired and want to go to bed, make an effort to get the kids to bed and spend a little time on the sofa together.

When you are looking at ways to spend longer together, and you have children, it becomes more difficult. It's not always possible to go to the movies or out for dinner once a week. If you have family close by then use them. If you can make it once a week, that's great, if not try doing something at least once a month that is just the two of you.

If you do go out for dinner every week, spice it up a little. Don't go to the same place, or eat the same type of food. If you are always doing the same, it can become a routine chore instead of your special time together. Look for new activities, go to a restaurant with live music, go bowling. Think of your first few dates, what things did you do together.

Plan some goals together. Holidays are a great place to start. Look at locations you want to go to as a family. Make a plan for your dream holiday to come true. This is a great motivation for you both, and it's something you can both invest in.

Make sure anniversaries and birthdays are celebrated with importance and meaning. I love birthdays, especially when you have children. I make a cake, I blow up balloons, I make an effort. This shouldn't just be left for the kids. Make an effort for your partner so that he can see he is loved. Use your anniversary as an excuse to get a night away together. It's one night a year! Don't feel guilty. You both work hard and deserve a treat.

Now we can't possibly discuss ways to develop a stronger, better, and deeper relationship without talking about sex. Blush if want ladies (and gents), but let's face it- Sex is awesome! And if it isn't, you need to fix this right away.

Psychologically, sex improves our self-esteem, reduces stress and anxiety. Physically, sex lowers blood pleasure, reduces the risk of heart attacks, boosts your immune system, and can count as exercise. Okay, you aren't going to burn as many calories as running. But even "vanilla sex" burns an average of 3.6 calories per minute, and it's better for your knees!

And now for your relationship. Sex brings you closer together, both physically and emotionally. It's a level of intimacy that exposes you in a way that nobody else sees. It enhances the trust between you, and it's fun.

If you have reached a point where you feel like your sex life is a bit stale, you need to take the bull by the horns (so to speak) and do something about this. I know you are tired, and I know you want to sleep. But having sex will make you sleep better, improve your mind, and you will find yourself walking with a spring in your step.

Like many things in life, we are still learning. I consider myself quite lucky, and I have been able to experiment in the bedroom, but that doesn't mean to say there aren't things I still want to try. It's like going to the same restaurant every week, in the end; sex is going to become boring.

Consider these ideas to bring your sex life back to life:

• Do some research, use the Internet for inspiration and find some things you want to try. If this is all new to you and you feel a little embarrassed about telling your partner what you want, send him a message. It's a great way to spice up your day.

• Don't feel like you aren't good at satisfying your partner if they have ideas that they want to try.

• Treat yourself to a sex toy. For some reason there is a stigma about sex toys, they are only good for single women or that it's because their man doesn't satisfy them. This is far from the truth. A sex toy can add a whole new dimension to your sex life.

• Don't restrict sex to the bed and before falling asleep. When you first got together, you may have wanted to have sex anywhere and everywhere.

• Forget about your inhibitions- you feel fat; get over it because you are beautiful. You feel embarrassed taking control, don't; your partner will love it. You are mortified at the idea of your husband spanking you; do you think you are the only person in the world who wants to try this?

• Laugh- when things go wrong, or you fall in a heap when a position doesn't work, laugh about it. I hate to use this pun, but get back on the horse and try again!

Your relationship has to last through major ups and downs, through stressful moments and joyful occasions. When your children are all grown up and leave the nest, it's just going to be the two of you. Make sure you keep working on your relationship in order to enjoy the love between you.

Up to now, I have covered our work, our home, our children, and our partners. The final chapter is going to be all about you. I've saved the best for last because without taking time to look after yourself, none of the rest would be possible.

CHAPTER 9. DON'T FORGET ABOUT YOURSELF - FOLLOW THE 3FS RULE

After everything you manage to do in a day, in a week, in a month, in a year, you deserve to think about yourself. I have said this before, but it is well worth reiterating, thinking about yourself is not selfish. It is necessary.

Once again, imagine your family as the staff. If the boss is happy, the team is happy. If mom is happy, the family is happy. For mom to be happy, you need to dedicate a little bit of time to your needs. Yes, this means more time, but it is crucial in order for you to feel better about life and to be able to handle all of the responsibilities you face.

So what are the 3Fs?

• Feel Good

• Follow your passions

• Find time for yourself

Much of what you read in this section will be a summary of what you have already read, but with more of a focus on you. It's also well worth reading it twice so that the idea of looking after yourself reminds you that you aren't neglecting your other responsibilities.

Feel Good.

You know this from moments in your past, when you feel good you feel like nothing can stop you, you are on fire, like an unstoppable machine. Negatives and problems come your way, and you solve them like a pro. At this moment you are on top of the world, and nothing can stop you.

This is the mentality we want to achieve on a regular basis. Not every single day because we are only human, but the majority of the time you need to be a powerhouse. How are you going to do this? By looking after yourself both mentally and physically.

You need to have a clear mind rather than the washing machine that doesn't stop spinning. Having a full mind has a negative impact on your outlook of life, and it can lead to problems sleeping. Once you can't sleep, a vicious cycle begins to form.

Keep a journal, practice meditation, go for a walk, spend time away from your phone, right lists of all the things you need to do. Be smart and realistic about your lists to ensure you achieve the things you need to do and to achieve the feeling of success.

Don't keep your emotions bottled up. Talk to people about how you are feeling. Don't waste time complaining about problems, it rarely achieves anything. Talk about problems with the aim of finding solutions and use people to help you see things from other points of view.

If you are the type of person who struggles to talk about their feelings, then this is when you need to keep a journal. While you won't get any feedback, it will certainly help you organize your thoughts and gain a deeper understanding of your feelings.

When you are mind is clear, you will find it much easier to stay focused. It will also help you handle all of the things you need to do.

To feel good, you also need to stay physically healthy. Tiredness, exhaustion, and illnesses are going to have a terrible effect on your time management. You need to get the amount of sleep your body needs. Most medical professionals suggest 7-8 hours of sleep per night, but it does greatly depend on the person.

Your diet will impact your energy levels, and you can never have too much energy! Work towards having a balanced diet, start the day with green tea or lemon, and hot water to cleanse your body. Don't skip meals, it's a devil for your metabolism. And don't be afraid of treating yourself to the odd fast food meal or chocolate donut.

Exercise may seem like a chore, but I promise you, it will only take a few days to start noticing the benefits. You will sleep better, you will have more energy, and you will feel better about yourself all-round. As more oxygen gets pumped to your brain, you will improve your level of focus and concentration.

Not everyone can go to the gym or sign up for a class. That's ok. We can start off with baby steps, 10-minutes a day. Go for a walk, dance, follow exercise routines from online videos. You will notice that once you get into a new exercise routine, you will be able to increase the level of activity and the duration.

Follow Your Passion.

A young student once told me that her mom's hobby was cleaning. It was adorable, but it also pointed out that our children often see us as robots rather than humans. How you act now teaches your children so much and lays the foundations for their future.

Hobbies and personal interests are necessary for individuals. It provides you with time to disconnect from the world of stress. It allows you to improve yourself, and it teaches you new skills you can pass on to your children.

Your hobby or your passion has to come from you. If your kids like swimming, going swimming with them isn't your hobby. The best way to rekindle your passions is to remember the person you were before responsibilities started getting on top of you.

When you were in your late teens or early 20s, what did you absolutely love to do? It doesn't have to be a typical hobby, like reading or riding a bike. I used to love doing cross-stitch. I found it relaxing, and I was proud of my creativity.

Talk to family and old friends who can remind you of what you used to like. It could be something as simple as listening to the music that used to motivate you when you were younger.

Your passion needs to include your future. What are your dreams and your desires? These things can be small, like to learn how to ballroom dance, or bigger, like a new house. Make a plan for how you are going to achieve your goals.

Don't just think of something you want and assume that because you want it badly enough, it will happen. You need a step-by-step plan to get there. Write it down and include each step and what needs to be done to accomplish it. You will find that once the bigger goals are broken down into smaller steps, they will become easier to envision. Take, for example, a goal to set up your own business:

• Decide on the business activity, can you do it from home, will you need a location

• Do the research, what other business are in the area with a similar product or service, who are your potential clients

• Make a business plan. Include set up costs, monthly costs, monthly income, the potential for growth

• Do you need finance to set up your business, what are the requirements

• Does your family agree? Do you have support from your partner and children?

Whatever your goal or passion is, have it written down and keep it close to you where you can see it. These dreams are what will motivate you to get through the more mundane jobs we have to do. I really want a new computer. I know that I need x amount of students with x amount of weekly classes in order to get my computer. Each class I teach brings me one step closer to my goal.

Find Time for Yourself.

Remember when your newborn baby fell asleep, and you had that precious time to yourself. What did you do? Read a book? Have a little nap? No! Like most of us, you probably ran around like a headless chicken trying to get a load of things done.

Being alone does not equal time for yourself. Finding time for yourself does not equal getting some cleaning down.

Time for yourself is time for you to do what you want to do. Whether that's to nosey through Facebook, read a book, go for a run, see your friends, anything but the activity must make you happy.

Yes, I know, a clean house makes you happy. But if you are following the steps in this book, you will have factored cleaning into your plans, and there should be an allocated time slot for this. Now it's time to allocate time for you.

Before you decide on the when and how to explain to your family that this time is for you and the reasons why you need it. Don't come across as if you need time away from them as you risk them feeling like they are your burden.

If you find the concept of taking time for yourself hard, start off with very short periods of time. 5 minutes might not seem like a lot, but it is time for you to jot some feelings down in your journal or do a few yoga poses. Once you feel comfortable, you will be able to extend the time for a bit longer.

Before you enjoy your alone time, make sure the family is all organized. Nobody is starving, and they each have things they can be getting on with. If you tell your family you are going to be 10 minutes, be 10 minutes. If it's an hour, tell them you will be an hour. Don't say 10 minutes and take an hour. The next time you say 10 minutes, they won't believe you.

Get a few of your jobs done and leave the house relatively clean and tidy. This way, you can enjoy your time more knowing that you have left everything under control, and it reduces the feeling of guilt.

Make the most of this time you have. I have said this many

times, but unless it's something you really feel like doing, stay away from your mobile. You might be tempted to have a quick look on Instagram, but before you know it, all of your time has been wasted watching silly videos.

Treat Yourself.

You are gradually becoming a time management queen. You are exercising more, you feel more productive, and the routine in the home is paying off for everyone. You work hard to comply with all of your responsibilities. Why on earth shouldn't you treat yourself for this?

Some man's heaven is another man's hell and not a truer word a can be said about rewards. What is a treat for me might be hell for you. The idea of going to a beauty salon for me is a nightmare.

My weekly Sunday treat is a glass of wine and a peel-off facemask. While my facemask is doing its magic, I may go all out and paint my nails. It may not sound much to you, but for me, it's the perfect way to reward myself for the week's efforts.

Maybe you want new shoes; maybe it's to buy something for your home. It might be a movie or a trip to the museum. For smaller achievements, reward yourself with smaller treats, for the bigger success in your week or month, go all out. Don't let family members steal away bits of your treat. Teach them how to make a to-do list, complete it, and think of their own treat.

Rewarding yourself for your successes is a great way of motivating yourself to work towards the next set of challenges. My facemask on a Sunday is like removing all of the stress from the week and preparing myself to start again on a Monday.

Regardless of your achievement and the reward you choose, it has to be done in the moment. Giving yourself an I.O.U treat doesn't work, as you will end up forgetting about it. One I.O.U treat becomes two and then 5. And most importantly of all, don't feel guilty.

CONCLUSION

I feel buzzed. One of my life goals was to write a book with some of my experiences in order to help others. I hope you realize that I am not a fat old man or inexperienced student writing a book from a bit of Google research in order to earn a quick buck. I am a 36-year-old self-employed mother of two. With my hand on my heart, every experience I have written about is true.

Not so long ago I was depressed, distant from my older daughter, convinced I was failing my baby, and on the brink of separation. I couldn't see a way of getting everything done and keeping everyone happy.

I searched through loads of methods and read books, but nothing really hit the nail on the head. I felt like I could implement one or two things here and there, but I didn't feel like I was making enough difference. I was frustrated because I was wasting time trying to find a solution.

Time management is a complex set of influences that combine multiple roles and responsibilities. You need to work, be a mom, a partner, you need to keep the home clean, your boss happy, your clients content. It's easy for all of these to get on top of you.

This book has covered a number of ways that you can start making small steps in order to achieve great results that will last. Here is a summary of some of the most crucial things that made a difference for me in a short period of time, even just days:

1. Go back to the basics. Decide on your dreams, your goals, and your passions. Remind yourself of who you were before the roles you have now

2. Make a plan. A long-term plan will help to motivate you to achieve bigger goals. Smaller plans are ways of making your goals more attainable.

3. Write to-do lists, wisely. Plan your day to maximize the time you have. Choose the times when you are more productive to do the tasks that require more concentration. Balance your day with easier and more difficult tasks, longer and shorter jobs. Keep the lists realistic.

4. When you are doing one activity, dedicate your time to that activity. Multitasking doesn't benefit you. If you are

bathing the kids, be there 100%, enjoy that moment, the same for time with your partner and yourself.

5. Learn how to say no and how to delegate. You don't need to do everything yourself. Whether it's your staff or your family members, they will appreciate the opportunity you are giving them.

6. Create a home where equality is the key. Everybody needs to pitch in to help with chores. There are many ways you can save time, especially when preparing meals. Seriously, consider that slow cooker!

7. Focus on yourself, your mental health and your physical health. Start off with small steps but start today- just 10 minutes for a walk around the block.

8. Spend quality time with your children. This might be from making conversation in car journeys or having a cuddle and a story. The older they get, the more difficult it is to spend time with them, but it is still necessary to have open and trusting relationships with your children.

9. Learn to love your partner again. Healthy conflict is good for your relationship. Communication is critical if you want your love to last the duration. Enjoy the time you spend together, and don't forget the importance of physical contact.

10. Don't feel guilty. Not for the bar of chocolate you eat, the glass of wine you drink, the hour you take for yourself. If you have completed your list, if you have worked all day

and everyone has eaten a healthy home-cooked meal, you have won! Reward yourself for the efforts you make.

On a final note, we are only human, and we make mistakes. The important thing is that we say sorry when necessary and lean from them. I can confidently say that even now that I have my daily plans, I know my goals, I organize my time well, I exercise, all the things I have written about, there are still days when I don't succeed. This doesn't mean that my system doesn't work; it means I am human. It's not your fault; you had a bad day.

Don't punish yourself for this, as there are some things in this world that we can't control. The important thing is you pick yourself up, dust yourself off, and start the next day knowing that you can achieve great things.

REFERENCES

Blake, W. (1863). *Auguries of Innocence*. unpublished: Life of William Blake.

David Allen Company. (n.d.). gettingthingsdone.com. Retrieved from https://gettingthingsdone.com/

DK. (2008). *The Cooking Book*. London: DK.

francescocirillo.com. (n.d.). Retrieved from https://francescocirillo.com/pages/pomodoro-technique

Gungor, M. (2012, October 31). YouTube; positive psychology [Video]. Retrieved from https://www.youtube.com/watch?v=29JPnJSmDs0

Harbinger, J. (2019, November). www.Inc.com [Blog post]. Retrieved from https://www.inc.com/jordan-harbinger/dale-carnegie-was-right-smiling-changes-everything.html

Jeevan, S. (2016, January 22). www.quora.com [Blog comment]. Retrieved from https://www.quora.com/What-are-the-most-surprising-real-life-examples-of-the-Pareto-Principle-the-so-called-%E2%80%9C80-20-rule%E2%80%9D

Ketchum, D. (2018, March 27). www.livestrong.com [Blog post]. Retrieved from https://www.livestrong.com/article/467052-does-cardio-give-you-energy/

Lusinski, N. (2018, February 22). 7 Ways Arguing Benefits Your Relationship, According To Experts. Retrieved November 7, 2019, from https://www.bustle.com/p/7-ways-arguing-benefits-your-relationship-according-to-experts-8268192

National Sleep Foundation. (2019). www.sleepfoundation.org. Retrieved from https://www.sleepfoundation.org/articles/how-does-exercise-help-those-chronic-insomnia

Time. (n.d.). https://time.com. Retrieved November 7, 2019, from https://time.com/4891579/how-many-calories-does-sex-burn/

Women's Health. (2018, September 8). maverdoctors.io [Blog post]. Retrieved from https://mavendoctors.io/women/fitness/10-minute-workouts-three-times-a-day-for-better-health-UewVtDGoik2HclH6qDAXLQ/

CLUTTER-FREE HOME

HOW TO DECLUTTER, ORGANIZE AND
CLEAN YOUR HOUSE IN 15 MINUTES
A DAY

INTRODUCTION

Clutter.

Some people believe it's a part of life. But others know that there is usually more clutter than what's needed. If you feel bogged down by all the clutter in your home and want to make your space better, like something out of an Instagram post, then you're in the right place.

In this book, we'll teach you how to confront the clutter, take care of it, and create a cleaner, more beautiful home than ever before.

However, how do you do it? How can you declutter your space, and keep it decluttered no matter what?

Well, the solution is in this book.

In this, you'll get solutions that allow you to break through all these struggles you have, and get the clutter gone for good!

In this book, you'll learn everything that you need to know about organizing and decluttering your home, especially if you're a busy home. No matter how many soccer practices you need to go to, or how many business meetings you have, we'll tell you how to declutter your space, and how to keep everything in order in just 10-15 minutes a day!

Yes, this is a decluttering book for the busy people in all of us, a set of solutions that will tell you immediately how to go about decluttering your space, so you're happy, and you don't feel overwhelmed by everything in your home.

The Problem

Being able to keep a space clean is very hard. I personally understand the struggle of keeping a space clean and making it stay clean. It's hard, and if you don't have ample time, spending your free days cleaning sounds awful.

But there is a solution to this, and I'll tell you how.

The Solution

The solution to this is simple: a little bit of cleaning each day goes a long way, and in this book, I'll tell you about the small steps you need to take to clean your space, but also how to do it, so you're not spending your days just cleaning.

Cleaning is boring, and decluttering can be overwhelming, but I'll tell you exactly what it is that you need to do, and everything in place that you should do to keep your space clean, and beautiful. When it comes to cleaning your home, it is possible to make the space clean and usable, no matter what.

My Story

I used to be like you. I worked a full-time job, and I have kids. That alone makes it a nightmare to clean. Every chance I had to clean, I wouldn't do it, because obviously, who wants to spend their days cleaning? I sure don't, and I'm sure you don't want to either.

But, when I learned that it's possible to declutter your home, make it look like something out of a Pinterest post, I grew excited. I decided to try it, and boy was I happy with the results.

I tried all of these different decluttering techniques, working from the easiest over to the hardest ones. I learned how to properly get rid of all the clutter in my home, and also, how to clean it so I felt happy with the results.

This is something everyone can get on board with. For most of us, it's obviously a struggle, and it can be hard for you to start. Trust me, when I sat down and started the decluttering process, I thought I was going to have a heart attack trying to get everything organized. But I learned how to do this effectively, and how to easily create a better home not just for myself, but for my family too.

If you're someone who doesn't like to clean, who would

rather sit around than clean your home, I get that. But, do you want to spend your time in a space that's filled with clutter?

Trust me, you don't want to be one of those people on Hoarders, that's for sure. While I'm sure it's not that bad if you keep putting it off, it's just going to make you feel terrible, and you won't want to do anything about it.

The hardest part is starting. I learned when I first did this, starting on this path was hard for me, simply because it required me to face my fears, to actually do something about all the clutter in my home. I had to sit there and be realistic, understand that some stuff was better off tossed, and I also learned that it isn't bad to throw away things you don't need.

I had to get through this hurdle before I even had a chance to do something about it, and I encourage you as a person to sit down, and realistically look at what you need, what you don't need, and to toss away the stuff that isn't worth it.

Because here's the reality of it: not everything needs to be kept. There are things better off left on the side or donated to another person. Some people can benefit from your stuff.

And there are things that are better left tossed in the garbage. We'll go over as well why people hold onto these material objects so much, and how to overcome your fear of keeping objects, so you're able to, with all of these as well, understand and do something about this. For most of us, when we start to learn and understand why we keep the items that we do, we'll be happier and much better off.

For many of us, learning how to better ourselves, and to create a space that we can use is vital. I do think it's time that you stop sitting around and avoiding it and start doing something about it.

Start Decluttering Today!

If you're stuck on how to start decluttering, then look no further. I'll help you with tips and tricks on how to declutter, and how to start doing it today, so you can have a cleaner tomorrow!

PART 1: DECLUTTERING

CHAPTER 1: ALL ABOUT DECLUTTERING

First, let's talk about decluttering. Before you can organize your space, you must declutter it. Here, we'll talk about decluttering, and the mindset for decluttering.

So What Is It?

When you declutter your home, you're removing all of the items that you feel won't necessarily benefit you if you keep them around. For example, stuff that either has a higher cost than benefit, whether it's financial or time-waster or is just taking up extra space in your home.

For example, let's say you have five different winter coats. You live in a space where it gets to the point where you need to wear a winter coat only like two weeks out of the year. Do you need to have five different winter coats? Course not!

That means, that it's just taking up needless space in your home. By being there, it really isn't benefitting you.

This is basically getting rid of anything that isn't really benefitting your home, making you a lot happier, and you can enjoy life so much more.

But Isn't That Just Minimalism?

Nope. Minimalism and decluttering are two very different things. With minimalism, you are getting rid of anything that is in excess, and in general, is downsizing your home immensely.

So, even if you needed the five different winter coats, you still would keep one, cause you're literally keeping just the bare minimum.

The idea behind minimalism is to just keep the minimal, and in general, is getting rid of almost everything. Minimalism is good if you really want to get rid of everything, but it's the more extreme form of this.

Decluttering is just getting rid of things that aren't going to benefit you. It might not be items that don't "spark joy", but instead, it's items that you simply feel are better off given to others than sitting around in your home like a bump on the log.

Like for example, if you don't read books in paperback form, do you need a whole library of books? Or would they be better at a used bookstore, where you might get some cash for them, or if they can't take them, you give them to Goodwill so someone else can use them? That's the idea of decluttering.

It's basically taking all the stuff that you personally feel isn't necessary, and giving them to someone else. Minimalism is a more extreme form of this, and unless you feel like just torching everything you currently have, I suggest keeping the mindset of decluttering more than anything else.

The Best Mindset for Decluttering?

There are sometimes when you feel like you need to have the mindset of getting rid of everything when you declutter.

However, that isn't the case.

Decluttering isn't just tossing everything you feel is "garbage" and getting rid of it all. It's about being selective in what you choose to get rid of.

Decluttering helps teach you what is important to you, and lets you become more selective of what you keep around. You are choosing what will benefit you, and also what you'll actually use.

Utilization is a big part of this. Look at everything that you keep around, and from there, you can choose what works for you. If you don't think you're going to use something, then go ahead and toss it.

This is a hoarder mentality for some of us to possess. The reason being, that if we're so used to keeping everything, tossing it can be hard.

But, if decluttering is hard for you, you need to focus on whether or not it's really that important. Sure, that dress is nice, but when's the last time you wore it? When do you think you're going to wear it again? If you can't really figure out the answer to that, then that's the problem here. If you can't, then you should toss it.

This is something most people don't realize is a big part of it. For most of us, the idea of tossing stuff we don't need isn't all that hard. But there is sentimentality that goes along with it. Sometimes, you might feel like getting rid of stuff you're not using is bad.

It's not. It clears out your space and helps you figure out what you really want from your decluttered home.

Helps You with Understanding Tastes

One mindset (that is great for those who are really struggling with decluttered homes) is understanding your personal tastes. Personal tastes change. What you liked a year ago might be different now. This is especially true with clothes, or even accessories and collectibles.

If you notice you're still collecting old things that you don't even like, one of the mentalities that you should have when decluttering is understand that things change. You're allowed to have a different mindset and a different taste for everything that you do. If you feel like you're really not going to benefit from this, then you should definitely just get rid of it.

There are many different benefits to decluttering, and understanding that it will help with getting the space in order is a big part.

Less Stuff, More Space

The biggest benefit of decluttering is the amount of space this gives you. Do you feel like you're grappling with having too much stuff? That's a sign you've got to declutter your space.

If you're so cluttered that you feel obstructed in your path in any way that's hazardous and irritating, you should declutter it.

But it isn't just a physical distraction, but also mental distractions. Do you sometimes look at spaces and feel very distracted by the space, simply because there is so much going on? That's the clutter that's there. You should keep yourself more disciplined and less distracted by decluttering. Sometimes, adopting the mindset of this gives you more space, and less desire to be distracted is one of the main reasons to adopt a decluttering mindset. You won't feel as pressured about cleaning, or feel as bad that you haven't, and essentially, you're putting a better foot forward, and you're not bogged down by your stuff.

Decluttering your space is very hard, and it can be a nightmare to do. But, if you know how to do it, then you'll be happier, and understanding what it is exactly, and why you should do it, along with the appropriate mindset for it, will help as well.

CHAPTER 2: THE PERFECT MOMENT TO START DECLUTTERING

So what is the perfect time to start decluttering? The obvious answer is right now, but is there a better time than right now to start decluttering? Well, lets' talk about how to start decluttering, and how to avoid the declutter paralysis that many individuals go through.

Spring Has Sprung!

Spring is probably the best time for decluttering. That's because it's in between both the hot season and the colder seasons. You've just got done with all the holidays, so you probably have a better idea of what was used and what wasn't used during the holiday season. Another part of that is the clothing you have too.

During the spring, you can accurately look at exactly what

jackets you wore during the winter, what excess items you never even touched, and various items that you feel just won't be used. You can also use this as a way to forecast your style for summer. For example, you can realistically look at your collection of summer dresses, and from there, you can decide whether or not it's needed.

Many people like to do this too because of the changing weather. Gone are the days of you sitting inside your home all the time, but instead you're getting out, enjoying the weather, and everything that's going on. It usually means it's nicer to stay outside, and much nicer for you weather-wise too. So, if you need to declutter your outdoor space, this is when to do it.

You can also look at various toys and other items your family has, and toss them away as well. You can look at everything and decide whether or not it will benefit you this coming year, whether it will help you relax, whether it will provide meaningful entertainment if you don't think it can, then there you go. It's not worth it.

But Shouldn't You Do It Now?

Yes, now is the ideal time. If you can, you'll probably want to start right away, but you have to feel that it's genuinely for you, that you will continue with this.

Look at your schedule and figure out whether or not it's possible to declutter during this time. Sometimes, the warmer months are a little easier for decluttering, since you'll have the drive to start, and you'll want to get going.

It also depends on your biological calendar as well. Are you the type who is more productive during the winter months rather than the summer? Then maybe decluttering in these months works for you! But you also run into the hurdle of Christmas and holidays, where you tend to get items, and it's hard to fully break away from that.

Nevertheless, you can start right now, and I encourage you to start as early as you can. But, understand it can be hard for some of us, but worth it at the end of the day if we can overcome these hurdles.

Decluttering Paralysis

This happens when you're trying to start, but you feel almost stuck or guilty because you don't want to get rid of it.

There are a couple of ways to handle it. If you notice that it's happening, you should consider the two questions that are below:

First, ask why you're trying to declutter. What the heck is your reason to declutter? Will it make you feel less stressed? Will you invite more people over and feel less ashamed if you have a decluttered home? Sometimes, when we start, we feel stopped, because we don't know why.

Maybe your motivation is the Pinterest blogs you see with all the pretty homes put neatly together. If that's the case, then continue with that energy. Understanding why decluttering is important to you as a person will help with this. If you notice you're struggling to let go of stuff, you need to sit down and understand that as well.

The idea of letting go is hard. This is something we'll touch upon in a later chapter, but if you do notice a paralysis in certain places you're working to declutter, figure out the why behind it? Are you worried people won't take it? Do you think you're going to feel bad if you keep it? That is a valid thing, but you need to sit down, and understand why you're stressed out about keeping it, and how to get over that stress when you declutter the home.

Holding onto clutter will keep you from getting past the struggles of a cluttered home. You'll be shocked at how easy it is to overcome the struggles of clutter if you know what you're doing and make the changes.

You'll also feel more inspired. If you feel paralyzed in the clutter too, work on spaces that are small, and you can picture how you want the space to look when you finish decluttering and organizing, and figure out how this will make you feel. You'll notice you're much more peaceful, and less overwhelmed if you're working in a home that's less cluttered.

So when is the best time to declutter your home? That answer is ultimately up to you. Figure out for yourself the best time to do this, and the best course of action to take. Understanding and mastering this will help prevent the paralysis and make your life so much easier for you as well.

Take the time to understand what's holding you back.

CHAPTER 3: DECLUTTERING TIPS, TRICKS, AND HACKS

Now that we've mentioned what it takes to start, let's talk about some of the hacks to make it possible for you to do it. Decluttering your home does take a little bit of time, dedication, and understanding to really do it right.

Start with One Bag of Clothing

First, start with one bag of clothing that you don't wear anymore, for one particular reason. Pick one part of your closet, and look at every item that's in there. Think about whether or not it fits. If it doesn't, then there you go, toss it. If you don't like the style of it, there you go, get rid of it again, or if you don't see yourself wearing it again, then put it in the bag. Fill it up, put it in your trunk, and then drop it off at a donation center next time you're by one. The best way to approach this is to take one place at a time and look at all the clothes you don't wear. As you do it, you'll realize that you'll have more pace, and it's much more suitable than letting it sit there too.

Paper Spots

Paper is one of the most popular sources of clutter. Think about all the papers you get from bills, general mail pieces, coupons, or whatever. If you notice that you're getting a lot of excess paper, you probably put them in so many places. You probably have them on the table, on the counter, in a drawer, on top of a dresser, and pretty much anywhere that isn't one singular spot. If you're someone that keeps losing papers, especially school papers, literally just put it all in one place. Designate one spot for this, and once a week, go through and figure out if you need them. Those expired coupons don't need to be held onto, and you'll realize that, once you get rid of things, life gets a little easier.

Create the Declutter Zones

Declutter zones are essentially the space that you determine that will never have clutter, whether it be a kitchen counter, a table, or even just an area around the couch. The idea behind this is simple: everything that's there will never be clutter you don't use. You should always keep this there and just put it away each time. Once you start to do this, expand this until it becomes the entire house. But you should keep everything simple in your space. Even just using one space to confront the declutter, and then move from this will help immensely.

Clean One Surface at a Time

One mistake I see so many people make is they will go and take on their entire home without realizing that if they do it all at once, they're going to get overwhelmed. What you do is pick one surface.

Personally, I like to start with the counters. This is great because it takes away the clutter from the flat spaces. For example, let's take the kitchen counter. Only keep the necessary appliances on there, and maybe one decorative candle. You should from there look at every single appliance that you have.

If you're not using your waffle maker frequently, then why is it on there? If you're not making blended smoothies, then get rid of it, whether it be storing it on a shelf or even just donating to goodwill. What you need to figure out is how to create a way for you to have spaces that aren't filled with items.

This can even work on non-kitchen surfaces. You don't need to have a stack of magazines on your coffee table, instead, maybe keep one there for decoration, and that's it.

You can do this with shelves too. Whether it's a shelf in a closet, bookshelf, or whatever, you just pick one shelf and work with it. Don't do the whole bookshelf in one moment either, but take literally one shelf, and then clear off any unnecessary items, so it looks clutter-free and neat.

Start Visualizing

When you are decluttering, think about all those rooms that you see and what you want them to look like. Which pieces of furniture do you want? What doesn't belong here but has gravitated towards this spot? What other flat surfaces do you want to clean up? If you start with each little space, choosing one at a time, and going from there, you figure out the essentials, and from this point, get rid of the rest of it.

The visualization helps you with putting an idea out there, and from there, you'll start to understand just what you need in order to help declutter your home.

The 30 Day List

The 30-day list is a simple solution for those of us who get tempted to buy new things as soon as we start decluttering.

You're probably guilty of this. You've spent all that time decluttering, and now, you want to buy a bunch of stuff. Maybe a "treat yourself" gift of a MacBook air or more books for the shelf. The best thing to do is you want to create a 30-day list. Every time you want to buy a thing that isn't totally necessary, what you do is throw it on the list. From there, you keep it there, and if it's been on the list for 30 days, buy it.

However, if you don't want to buy it anymore, scratch it off the list. This is a crazy thing that totally works because you'll notice over time that the urge to buy items will start to go away, and you'll save yourself both money and space. This is super effective and wonderful for those of us who are guilty of impulse buys.

Simple Folder sand Filing Finally, start to file and create folders for everything. These pile up high, and you should create some folders with different labels on them, for both the simple paperwork and the major bills. Have everything in one specific spot, and when the system is there, you just file this easily. It doesn't have to be perfect, so if you have extra labels there, put them on, and then there you go.

You should also set up a simple filing system as well, and from here, take a handful and work with them. Make very quick decisions and don't ruminate on that one. Once the system is in place, you file as needed, and make a note of the actions you need to. Don't put anything back into the pile, but work with it. If you can't do anything with it, and if you don't think it's a necessary piece of paper, simply toss it.

Hanging About

If you have clothes that you're never wearing, what you should do, is every time you wear something, change the side of the hanger. For example, have them all hang with the edge of it sitting out, and from there, when used, you flip it. Continue to do that, and after a year, if you realize you never touched some of the dresses you have, you should from there get rid of them.

If they are seasonable clothes, put them in a box, and if you notice that you never touched the box, then just get rid of them period.

These hacks are the best way to go about decluttering the space. I get that decluttering is hard, it's definitely not a simple thing for any of us, but with the proper care, and the right steps, it's possible.

CHAPTER 4: OVERCOMING THE GUILT OF DECLUTTERING IN JUST A FEW MINUTES

It happens to the best of us. We find items that we have sentimental attachment towards, and we feel bad for tossing them. This is something that happens to many of us more often than we think, but these emotions won't go away. Here, we'll discuss the best way to cope with this and how to deal with the emotions at hand.

Why Does It Happen?

Decluttering guilt happens because, when you start to declutter, you come to the realization that you have a lot of unnecessary stuff.

You start to wonder whether you should hold onto it for the simple reason, you might use it again in the future.

This type of guilt happens because people feel bad for

getting rid of things. This especially happens if you have a lot of perfectly cleaned and useful things.

Sure they might be useful to someone else, but when's the last time you used them.

This guilt does tie into the decluttering paralysis that occurs when you start cleaning. You feel guilty for doing this, even though the reality is, you're never going to use it.

The guilt can stop you from decluttering some spaces, and you might not be motivated to get rid of it.

What's the easiest way to rectify this situation then? Well, I know what I did, and I'll tell you how to do it.

How to Handle Decluttering Guilt

The best way to do it is to have the motivation to declutter. Why are you doing it? Look at why decluttering this will benefit you, and if you need to, stop and list out the benefits of decluttering, and how to handle it.

When you declutter, keep that motivation, and keep that energy going. It will handle the issues that come up when you declutter and feel less guilty much.

When you do feel guilty about abandoning items, look at why that is? Is it because you fear getting rid of items? Do you think there might be a reason for keeping it that's eating away at you? Do you feel bothered when you get rid of items? Look at the exact science behind why you feel guilty exactly, and why it is eating away at you. Once you do that, you'll start to realize that it's just the past making you feel guilty.

If it's something that you bought with someone that has emotional ties to it, sit there and realistically look at whether or not that will benefit you, and whether or not you should even keep it. As well, think about whether or not you're going to use this.

I had this issue with a blender I got. It was a gift from my parents for my wedding, and that, along with many of the other household items had sentimental value to them, even though they were just material things. I looked at this, and I thought to myself whether or not this is better kept or tossed. I realized the reason I felt guilty about this wasn't that I was afraid to toss it, but I felt guilty getting rid of items my parents had given to me.

But, when I looked at how much I'd use it, or even if it was worth keeping around, I started to realize it's better to toss things you don't need, and better to get rid of them.

The guilt of decluttering is a real thing, and it's a frustrating thing to deal with, mostly because people don't realize that holding onto these items does make you feel almost bad. But, if you understand why you feel bad, and understand that feeling guilty will only hang around if you don't get rid of it, it can help with the hurdles you're going over, and the struggles of decluttering.

CHAPTER 5: THE ROOM-BY-ROOM GUIDE TO DECLUTTERING

In this chapter, we'll highlight the exact strategies you need to take in order to declutter the space room-by-room, and how to handle every single room.

Living Room

First, let's talk about the living room. The best way to handle this is simple:

- Begin with the counters, clearing off the clutter there

- Look at the couch, and put away all items that don't belong there

- Fold blankets, and any that are old and ratty, you toss

- Look at gaming systems, and get rid of any clutter that's there, especially cables

- Clean off your entertainment system of anything that doesn't belong there, or anything you won't use

- If you have DVDs or CDs that you don't think you're going to use, toss them

- If there are any knickknacks that don't belong there, get rid of them right away

- Clear off any furniture that has stuff that you don't need there

- If you have excess furniture, consider tossing it or getting rid of it

- Clear off one shelf at a time, and make sure that they're neatly organized

- If you have bookshelves, clear off each shelf of any books that aren't necessary

Bedrooms

Bedrooms depend a lot on how you want them to look. Some people like a simple style for their bedrooms, others like it when you have more items around. Here, we'll talk about how to clear up bedrooms of clutter.

- Start with the closets, first and foremost going in, and finding all of the items you haven't worn in the last year. Try them on, and if you don't like how they fit, or they're too big or too small, you toss them

- Look at any extra items sitting in your drawers. If they

don't fit there, toss them or put them in the rightful place

- Look at socks and undergarments. Lots of us keep the old raggedy underwear and hosiery, so it's better if you just toss anything with holes in it

- Look at the different types of clothes you wear, especially jackets and coats. If you don't see yourself wearing them, then toss them

- For the bed, if you have too many pillows and excess things, get rid of them

- For drawers and vanities, get rid of anything that's too much on the counters, and either clear them off by putting them in their rightful place or toss them.

Kitchen

The kitchen can be hard to declutter quickly, but here, we'll highlight some of the best decluttering tasks for the kitchen:

- Take the stuff you don't use off the countertops

- Take a small shelf in the fridge, look at the items, and if you see anything you don't use, or can't eat, or it's expired, just toss it. Take one shelf at a time

- For the kitchen table, keep it uncluttered as much as you can, finding homes of everything on there that's possible

- For the cabinets, grab anything that's not needed, and just give it away or toss it.

- If you have lots of cups, look for any broken ones and toss those as needed

- On the floor, try to keep everything as neat as possible.

- For the pantry, keep items off the floor, and if you notice something hasn't been touched food-wise in over a month, get rid of it

Bathrooms

Decluttering the bathroom is quite easy, and here, we'll highlight the top things you've got to worry about when you're cleaning the bathroom:

- Clean the area under the sink, getting organizers and getting rid of any beauty products you don't use

- If you have makeup that's over a year old, toss it

- If you have beauty products that you don't use, toss them

- Look at the medicine cabinet, and if you have old prescriptions, toss these bad boys

- Look at any hair products, and if you know you and the family don't use them, either toss or give them away to someone who does

- Get rid of any clutter around the toilet, sink, and counters. Keep it minimal

- If you have a lot of toothbrushes or toothpaste, if they

aren't bad or look grungy, store them to a spot to use, and get rid of them if they're gross

- If you have empty shampoo and soap bottles or dispensers, either fill them up or toss them

Home Office

With the home office, this one might take a little bit longer, simply because of all the stuff you might have that you don' know what to do with. But here are a few tips for decluttering this area easily:

- Handle all the papers and put them in one area

- Sort all the papers, and never leave any of them unread

- Clear off the countertop of the office for only the essentials like a laptop, notepad with a plan, and so on

- If you have drawers, tackle one drawer at a time, and get rid of any papers stashed there, or any stuff that isn't necessary

- If you have any papers or items on your office furniture such as chairs and cushions, take them and put them in the rightful place

- Look at the bookshelf, and see if there are items that you don't need. If there are, simply get rid of them

- Do a sweep of your office every day, looking for any excess clutter, but not spending much time on the space

Craft Room

The craft room and playrooms tend to be messier than others, but here, we'll highlight some of the best ways to declutter this space, so it's meaningful

- If your child has outgrown the toys that they have, or they haven't touched them in a bit, put them in a box to donate, unless you have another kid who might grow into some of them

- Get any old crayons or other items and put them all neatly in a container to use

- If you have craft items, put them in an organizer or a shelf, and neatly go through them, see if you'll use any of it

- If you have lots of excess sewing scraps, if you know you can't use a scrap, then toss it. If you know you won't be making anything with it, then toss that as well

- If you have a messy counter for crafting, get rid of anything that you don't need

- Put any crafting tools in one specific area, and if any are broken, then get rid of them

- If you're using foam crafts, create one specific space for all the film, and from there, put it all in one singular location

Any Clothes

Clothes are harder, but there are a few ways to really clean up a clothing space, and here, we'll talk about that:

- If you have any clothes just sitting about, get them to the right space

- If an article of clothing has holes in it, get rid of it

- Take one drawer, one closet, one wardrobe at a time: don't try to organize all the spaces at once

- If you notice you have items you can't remember you last wore, you should toss them

- If nothing else, try the hanger technique

- If you have socks without mates and haven't found the mates, get rid of the socks

- If you can't think of a place to wear the items, then don't keep the item, just toss it

Storage

Finally, we have storage, which is hard cause you run into the "well maybe I'll use that" concept when looking through it. But here we'll highlight some decluttering you can do for a storage space, whether it's an attic or otherwise:

- If you haven't touched the item in the last five years, then toss it

- If you can't think of a use for this item, then toss it

- If you have seasonal clothes up there, go through it, and if you have multiples of a seasonal item you don't need, just toss it

- If you have old decorative items that you keep putting off of tossing, then it's better to toss them

- The only thing that might just be worthless or mostly sentimental that you keep are family heirlooms, but keep them off to the side so they're not mixed in

- If you have some boxes with house figurines or the like, keep them all in one box, that way it takes up less space

- Don't get hung up on keeping things you don't need when decluttering this space

Storage is probably harder than the other spaces, since most of the time the intent of storage items is to store them, but this is a good place to declutter.

Don't spend a lot of time on any of these locations, but instead, be aware of everything you're tossing, so you're able to, with this as well, toss all the items you don't need.

CHAPTER 6: SELL, DONATE, OR TRASH — WHAT DO YOU DO WITH IT?

This is something most people run into later on. They don't know whether they'll benefit by selling, donating, or trashing the items. If you're at a loss for what to do with this, then you should take some time to read this chapter and understand where to go with it.

When to Sell

The best time to sell is if the item is in near-perfect condition, but you don't have a use for it.

Some of us have clutter in the form of dresses with tags, items still in-box that we never opened, and just items that we kept around but never got around to doing anything with them.

These types of items are perfect for selling.

Now, you may wonder where you're supposed to sell these things. The best bet is to sell them in a place where people will more likely buy them . If you have time for a yard sale or want to collaborate with others on one giant yard sale, then great. Sometimes, flea markets, if you have any time to spend at these, might be good, or if you have family willing to help.

If you're okay with holding onto these for a bit, then throw it on eBay or Amazon. If you have a popular product, the supply and demand might be limited on it, so you could sell it for a pretty penny in response.

Selling is best when you have the item in place, but you don't need it, and you think it's better left with someone else.

When to Donate

The best time to donate items is if they are items that you don't feel like you're going to sell, or you don't have the time and desire to sell these items.

The best items to sell are usually the ones in near-mint condition, but if you have old clothing, stuff in older styles or just items that you don't think there's a demand for, donating is the best way to do it.

The best part about donating is it helps others. Goodwill, for example, has a very simple donation system. You don't even need to use goodwill to do this. There are different donation centers and thrift stores to choose, and if you want to use this means to donate, then, by all means, go for it.

For most of us, donating is an easier route. If you don't have the time to sell it on a site or have a garage sale, and if it's older items that you feel people don't want or just random stuff that you think might be better just donated, then this is the best plan for you. Plus, if you're helping charities, it's definitely not a bad thing.

When to Trash it!

Trashing is probably the last course of action you should take with your items.

If you can't donate it, then you trash it.

Trashed items are usually things that don't benefit anyone because they're old, such as in the case of old, rotten food, or raggedy undergarments and socks. Anything with holes in it is better off just trashed.

The thing about trashing, however, is if you can give it to someone else, that's better. I'm talking more from an environmental standpoint. For most of us, when we just trash it, it's going into a landfill, and some things aren't properly broken down.

If you can recycle it somehow, that's the better option. Old clothes make great cleaning rags.

But, if you're not sure, take it to the charity to donate. Sometimes, they'll take some things you were otherwise going to trash. For food pantries, if you have some food that hasn't gone bad, then you can donate it. But, if the expiration date is long gone, then you're going to have to trash it, no matter how useful it might be.

The "Maybe" Box

There is also the maybe box. This is something you should have on hand when you're going through stuff, and if it's something that you're not sure about whether to keep, trash, or donate, this is where you keep it. Sometimes, you have stuff that you dot use a lot, but you might need it eventually. If it gives you that thought that getting rid of it may not benefit you, this is where the maybe box comes in. This is a box that's kind of hidden so that you're not totally thinking about it all the time. The concept behind this is to see if you actually use this.

Now, when you're not organizing your space and use using it, if you think about this item, you should go over and grab it. From there, put a date on the box of six months from now. Six months later, look in the box, and pull out everything that's in there.

See if there is anything that you don't need from this. If you find some item that you know you'll use, maybe like a snowblower or a leaf blower during certain seasons, then keep it. Usually though, you'll then dump the whole box, because you never really needed it, and it's a good idea to have this around. From there, you can donate, sell, or trash it.

For most of the items that you have, a donation is a way to go. That's because, when you donate the item, someone else is going to get good use out of this. This also helps with the guilt you feel when you're getting rid of items. Sometimes, just thinking of the fact that someone else might benefit from this is enough to help you get rid of it. Plus, you're thinking about others, which is a good thing.

This is a big part of decluttering, and hopefully, you now have an idea of where to put all of the items that are there.

CHAPTER 7: KISS STRATEGY — HOW 10 MINUTES A DAY KEEPS THE CLUTTER AWAY!

This is an important part, and it's super simple to do. Keeping it simple is the way you declutter, and it can help make the whole process easier to take care of.

The reason why you have clutter is probably that you were a little lazy with putting stuff away. Sometimes you just leave something there and think "I'll do it later", but you never do it later.

Sometimes, we're all too busy with our lives, and if you work a job, chances are you don't want to sit around and worry about the nuances of how cluttered your house is. Most of us don't want to spend the time or the extra steps putting mail into the shredder or sorter, instead, we leave it lying on the counter.

We'll do this with everything. If we have a jacket, we wore

but don't need it now, we're more inclined to throw it on the floor or the couch, rather than put it away. Sometimes it might be because we're just hurrying from one part of the room to the next part, rather than actually looking at what we're doing and being mindful.

The idea behind decluttering is to get rid of the stuff you don't need, and from there, you put the rest in its rightful place. That's all it is, and that's how it should be.

While you might have some really deep and thoughtful process on decluttering, the best way to do it is KISS — Keep it Simple, Stupid.

This isn't an attempt to make you feel bad or belittle you, but instead, understand it doesn't take much to clean up your home.

For many of us, we think it takes forever, but it doesn't. Not when you've already put everything in place and work to clean it up.

Seriously, Keep It Simple

If nothing else, be simple with this. You can create small reminders on the various tasks, such as a sign that says, "Don't put clutter here!" and then tape this in the spot that people tend to leave cutter. Even just posting it on the fridge might be a good, gentle reminder.

Some people think they need to put together some complex color-coordinated system of keeping clutter away. That's fine and dandy if you want to go through those motions, but here's the thing: keeping it simple is the way to go.

If you do these complex systems, it won't create a habit. The goal here is a habit because that will, in turn, help you keep the space properly cleaned. If you don't form a habit, then you're going to have a rough time.

I like to figure out the easiest ways to do it. You know what they say: if you do it the laziest way, it requires the least work.

I'm not saying don't ever put your stuff away, but put it all in a place where, if possible, clutter says no.

Just Put Your Stuff Where It Belongs!

If nothing else, start putting stuff where it belongs. This is part of the simple solution to declutter and maintain an orderly home.

What this means is, instead of just throwing your coats, backpacks, or whatever all around like they're just some toy, take everything, and mindfully put it back where it came from.

I don't care if it is somewhere that you use a lot, or a place you rarely touch; just put it back where it belongs. Having a home for the items you need is so important that you'd be surprised at how effective it is to follow this.

Sometimes the Easiest Systems Work the Best

There are those of us who think that we need to make some methodical plan and deep schedule where we need to follow everything to the letter, and focus only on doing that.

No, you don't have to. Seriously, keep it simple, stupid.

One of the biggest mistakes you can make with decluttering your home is that you don't realize that if you try to use the hard and complicated systems, you just get very overwhelmed. What you need to do is put together the system that will help you out, and one that you'll keep.

The way to do it is pretty simple: if you have a room, pick a spot, declutter it, and don't move forward till that's finished. Do not pass go, do not collect 200. This keeps you focused, and if you keep it simple, it'll make things easy.

Start with One Thing at a Time

I'm sure you probably have a bunch of areas that need decluttering, but the easiest way to keep this simple is to just start with one area, and go from there. This is the easiest way to do it, simply because if you do this any other way, you're going to get overwhelmed, and you're not going to be happy.

What I like to do is work in one space, and then when I'm fully done with that, I work on another space. You might not even fully declutter one space in a day, and that's okay! The best thing to remember about all of this is that if you declutter it in this fashion, it'll be easier on you as well. Building your own personal plan to declutter it in just one step at a time is essential, and very important because otherwise, you'll get overwhelmed, and not happy.

The idea of taking this a step at a time might seem trite and boring to most people, and you might feel like you're on this forever, but you don't have to be. Your mindset is the other thing you also need to keep simple.

A Simple Mindset for a Simple Job

One part of KISS you have to understand is that while yes, it's physical, it's also a mental thing too. Don't sit there and try to get rid of stuff and think of all of the reasons to keep a dress you haven't worn at all in the last three years, just ask yourself if you've worn it, and if you can't say yes, then toss it.

"But what about"—If you don't see yourself using this or can't think of a reason to keep it, then toss it to the side.

This is a big one. The problem with most of us is we are thinking people. We could come up with a thousand reasons to keep that creepy collector's item that's stowed away in the back, but even you don't want to look at it, but that doesn't mean you have to do that.

The biggest thing to remember is that you need to keep a simple mentality along with a simple physical activity from it too. If you think you won't use it, then toss it. If you don't have an exact use or reason for this, then get rid of it. If you don't think you'll actually have a purpose for this, then why are you keeping this stuff around?

One part of setting and forgetting that we oftentimes forget about, and one of the biggest things to remember when cleaning up your space, is that you have the power to decide the fate of all of your items, no matter how big or how small they are. If you don't think you need it, you have to learn to let go. And sometimes the quick and dirty way of deciding this is more valuable than sitting here ruminating on why you should keep this thing you haven't touched in months.

The concept of a simple mindset for a simple job is something we need to adopt. If you do this in a way that's simple, you'll get through this faster, and you'll be happier too. This is a big thing to remember, and a big part of decluttering.

Know the Giveaway Items That You Can Toss Right Away

This one is important. If you already know of things that you don't need, then by all means, just toss these bad boys. Get rid of them like a bad apple.

If you have old, rotting food somewhere, get rid of it. If you have clothes that are too soiled to wear again, then toss them. If you have children's toys, that you know nobody in the house will use, then toss them. This is a big part of decluttering, and you have to remember that one of the biggest parts of decluttering is knowing what you need to toss and what's willing to be kept around.

When you do this, you'll realize that decluttering items for the trash is much easier than you think. People don't realize that this is the beginning of the process, and you have to keep this simple. To do otherwise will defeat the purpose of this, and if you don't take care of this now, it'll just pile up.

That's also a big part of keeping the space clean after decluttering. If that food's old, get that off the counter! If you know, you're not going to wear this again, either sell or donate. You don't need to get into the whys and wherefores of your stuff, just be smart, and start to toss anything that you know won't benefit your life anytime soon. It's good to be honest with yourself on this, but also know that, once it's over, you'll be happier with less stuff.

Keeping it simple is very important, and if you're not keeping it simple when decluttering, then what's the point? Getting out of the complexities of your head so you can throw away items you don't need is important and valuable for you as a person.

PART 2: ORGANIZING

CHAPTER 8: AFTER THE FALLOUT — HOW TO ORGANIZE WHAT'S LEFT

So you've finally gotten rid of all the stuff that you have, and now you're ready to organize. Congrats, and now, you'll learn every single step that's in place to teach you how to organize any part of your home, and how to do it effectively.

Organize Your Home into "Zones"

Zones are essentially how you divide a room. This makes the organizing of space less overwhelming, and it is a good way to sort other items that you have. If you have a kitchen, for example, you will have specific places for the supplies you need for baking, your cutlery, any staples, and also plates and cups. Having all of this in place is a form of organizing.

Another zone is the linen closet, where you'll have towels,

cleaning supplies, linens, basic household needs such as paper towels, and from there, you take stock of where these go, take such items and organize them based on each zone.

Focus on Accessibility

The idea behind this is the more an item is used, the easier it should be to access. What you have to do is to store the items that you use daily towards the front and more towards your eye level. The concept behind that is that if you need it, it's right there and you don't have to spend money purchasing that once again. If you have cupboards, get some of those small pull-out bins for this in order to make it accessible. The tiered shelving with the back visible is a good one too, and that's definitely a good idea for this.

You should also consider the location of where they're going, and try to store these in the area as much as you'll be using them, especially if it's a daily occurrence. Kids' storage areas for their supplies should, of course, be low and easily accessible.

Make It Easy to Look At

The one thing with organization is you need to make it so that you can actually use it, and that it's easy to look at. Sure, a card catalog filing system for everything might seem like a good idea at first, but if it's too organized, it feels almost tedious to keep up with. You should be able to look at it, see what you need, and then take your stuff out, and then put it back where it belongs when you're finished with the job. That's the ultimate goal of this, and what you should be going for as well. Understand that, and you'll understand the concept of organization.

Make it look pretty, but also, you know exactly where everything is in its own way, so you're able to, with this as well, put together the easiest shelving system, and process you can put together. Remember, you want to use this, right? Then make sure it can be usable.

Space Optimization

One part of this is to optimize the space for both function and storage. For example, hooks, bars, storage caddies, and those little carriages for projects to help make it work for you. Adding these to the closets on the sidewalls is good.

When you have tiny storage faces, think in a vertical manner, and add additional shelving to the higher up areas for the seasonal items, or those not as frequently used, or even a storage unit that's walled. The big thing to remember is to not be afraid to get creative with this and figure out the multi-use pieces that work for decoration, along with storage too. Figure out your space, how you want to use it, and the best way to apply this as well.

If you do this, you'll be able to use it, and in your own way so that you're happy with the results.

Again, Keep It Simple

This is again, simple to how decluttering is to, and you want to make sure that you want to keep it in a way that's simple for you to maintain. Keep it simple, and keep it in a way that you actually want to make it so that you're able to use this. You should make sure that you don't make it so that you have to move twenty other items in order to get to one box. That's silly, and you want to make sure that every item you have is accessible with one step.

For example, if you have a certain type of makeup you need then go get it. For items that you need less of, then keep it two steps to get it. The big thing to remember here is you don't want to move a bunch of stuff out of the way to just get one item. For those items that are less frequently used, the two steps rule is the way to go.

The idea is that the easier it is for you to grab it, the more it'll be used. And it'll also make it possible for your family to use it too. It's easier to get your husband to actually put away the dishes or the groceries if it's in a way that's easy for him to do, rather than some convoluted way that only benefits you, right?

Don't Buy Organization Bins at the Beginning

The big thing to remember with this one is that while those organization systems are wonderful to use, limit your purchase of them till after you're done with putting things away. Bins, baskets and the like are great for keeping your items nice and neat, and they're ideal for making everything tidy, but the thing is, you should try to buy all this at the end of the process because you want to enhance the organization, not build it around these items.

Having five storage bins is great, but did you really need those five when a small caddy holding everything could've sufficed? People don't realize this, and then, they end up wondering where all their money went. Well, it's because they were buying the organizational items instead of just organizing.

A lot of people who are trying to organize fast end up making this mistake, and it's a fatal error. It can end up ruining the entire process, and it can be quite cumbersome to you. So, it's in your best interest to make sure that, if you do use organization products, that's great, but you should also be willing to make sure to use other ways to organize your home as well.

Label It!

If you want to make it easy to use, use labels. People will know where to put things if it's got a nice label on it. Your family will thank you if you take the time to use labels on everything. This is incredibly helpful for trying to get into storage or reach the areas that are difficult to well, reach. If you know where to put something because of a fancy label, this reduces the instance of putting it in a basket that's random and thereby, also reducing the chance of people not putting stuff where it needs to go.

Evaluate and Modify

After you've started to organize, you should look at the space that you have, and see whether or not it can be adequately maintained. Very organized spaces will be easy to maintain with only a few minor additions or changes. If you notice that this space is starting to get cluttered again, look at it, and start to see if you have too much stuff in there. If the items, that are difficult to access, require multiple steps, and whether or not things are put back in the right spot or not. This last one is mostly just resolved by being more diligent about where you put your items.

The idea behind this is to tweak everything and get back to the drawing board with all of this and do this with space.

One thing to remember with decluttering is that it's a process that continuously happens. If you declutter a little, you need to organize a little bit more too. Sometimes you might need to declutter a little bit more, and then purchase a couple of bins for it, and put those away. Sometimes even decluttering to put items properly away is the best option for this too, and you should understand that, with organization, it will make a difference. You need to understand that organizing is a process, and it's something that you should try to work on bettering and mastering over time.

Don't Mass Organize Any Room

The big thing you've got to remember is that you should never declutter an entire space in one fell swoop. Start with a space, and then work from there. For example, start with maybe a cabinet, a shelf, or whatever, and after you've decluttered it, organize this bad boy. This will, in turn, help your home look better, and you won't get as overwhelmed.

You need to understand as well that doing this room by room in a tiny manner is better for those of us that have a busy schedule. After all, who wants to spend hours reorganizing their room?

I don't, and I don't think you want to either.

The best way to do this is to declutter slowly, and declutter and organize based on each space. Sometimes, you'll realize some places are better off with certain items than others, but understanding that you have to figure out the home for all your stuff is just as important too.

For rooms, you should always consider the way you organize each space and any shelving that's there for you to use.

How to Approach a Space

When looking at decluttering, what you need to do is first and foremost, look at each space you have, whether it be a drawer, a cabinet, or whatever. From there, picture how you want the room to look, including each and every different way to organize and make it easier to approach. From here, figure out the process you want to make this work. Then, you do it, and finally, you adjust, label, and put everything back as needed.

It's that easy, but you have to understand that it's definitely not easy for you to do, and sometimes when you organize, you'll realize it's hard to keep things all tidy. But, keep it simple stupid, and understand that, once you've finished a space, move onto the next one.

Now that you know how to organize spaces, you will now learn how to use different organization methods to clean up each room and organize it effectively.

CHAPTER 9: THE BEST IN-DEPTH GUIDE ON HOW TO ORGANIZE YOUR SPACE

So how do you organize a room in each space? Well, we're about to go through each and every single room and give you the exact tips, tricks, and ideas to help you clean up your space within each room.

Living Room

For the living room, there are a few ways to really keep it nice and tidy, and this section will discuss how you can keep your living rooms very orderly and inviting .

- Put a small, decorative wastebasket in your living room to help keep trash out of there as much as possible.

- Get a small little basket to put the magazines, papers, books, or brochures and make sure that you keep it clutter-free on every surface.

- If you have extra pillows and blankets, get a small basket, fold them up, and nicely put them next to the couch.

- Fluff every pillow at least once a week to help make them look nice and full.

- For entertainment systems, start to get cord organizers to help keep everything tidy around there.

- If you have game systems, neatly wrap the cords and put them into a small little basket to the right of where the consoles are.

- Wrap up all of the wires you have, neatly put a cord organizer on them, and from there, set them on the side. Having a plastic bucket is great for this.

- If you have any small knickknacks, try to reduce them from where the flat surfaces are in your home.

- Put either a small bookcase or a table with some storage bins underneath if you don't have a playroom for kids to sit in and enjoy everything, and you can add rolling toy bins to help keep everything there.

- Add rolling baskets or bins under your coffee table to help store the clutter such as remote controls, drink coasters, or even magazines.

- Keep a separate shelving area for games, and make sure to keep it neatly organized.

- Get an armoire that will house all of your games and

systems, and make sure that the surfaces are neatly organized.

- Consider hanging up your photos or even using a digital photo album rather than just throwing them on your coffee table or flat surface, since it will reduce your clutter, or you can keep them on the bookshelf in one location.

- You can also put the blankets and pillows behind the sofa or even the cabinet or bookcase if you feel like that's a better location for these items.

Bedrooms

Your bedrooms are the next location that you should consider looking into. As the closet is such a significant and large area, we'll discuss this later on, here are some organization tips that will help you put your bedroom into a rightful place.

- Consider using the area underneath your bed to store some of the different items that you need, such as gift wrap, linens for the room, or for kids bedrooms some extra books and toys

- Put your artwork on the wall, and don't leave it on the nightstand or dresser, and it will help keep a more streamlined appearance.

- Keep all of your flat surfaces as decluttered as possible, and try to keep a more cohesive look that's organized to your space.

- Consider a rack for your blankets, and install this rack right next to the bed. This is great if you have a lot of throws, quilts, and bedding that you don't really feel like putting away, and it makes turning the bed down easier. Plus, it does ultimately save a lot of floor space.

- Again, get some baskets for your pillows, and try to put them on a basket that's next to the bed. You can also, if you strip your bed down every night, put it all in there and grab it in the morning in order to help make it functional for everyone.

- Keep a night table that is functional with an organizer on that, or also a small dresser and some of the small little knickknacks and a lamp there. Try to make sure it's both functional and clutter-free as well.

- Have a hamper in every bedroom. That way, you won't have to worry about clothes not being washed or strewn all across the floor. You can get one that fits the home, or even just a basic hamper.

- If you dislike how the hamper looks, throw it in your closet. It keeps it out of your hair, and in turn, will help to make the space much easier to work with.

- Make sure every place has a garbage bin, your bedroom included. A small little pail works that you can throw right next to the nightstand is ideal. You can throw small pieces of trash, tissues, or scraps of paper into there, and it doesn't have to be something big and obnoxious, but rather, something small and functional.

Kitchen

The kitchen is the next disaster zone to tackle, and boy can it be terrible. Here are a few little tips to help you make it so that you can use your kitchen easily and effectively.

- Get rid of some of those plastic containers that are stained, won't fit together correctly, or have cracks. From there, stack by size, and from here use dividers to stash the lids, and then sort it by size for very easy visibility. Try to replace these slowly but surely with glass ones before the end of the year, since it is safer and easier for you to use as well.

- If you have a lot of plastic bags, get a small container, and put it into there. This is a canister that can be covered with cardstock, and from there, decorated to spell bags with letting. Roll your plastic bags into a small circle, and thread the first bag through there and pull it up. If done right, it will then start to move upwards as you grab one, and it beats having an entire cabinet of plastic bags, right?

- Clean out and organize your fridge. You should've already gotten rid of all the bad stuff, but now take some small containers and put these in there. Have everything in a place where it would make sense to be put. You can actually look at the different types of foods and organize it by that, use the most frequently used foods near the front, and try to use baking soda to clean your fridge down rather than actual cleaners, because you don't want that on your food.

- For the cabinets, try to maximize your cabinet space by putting stemware glasses upside down and look at your dishes, putting the more frequently used items near the bottom since that's, of course, more convenient. Try using the interior shelves too in order to accommodate the other dishes. Consider putting nesting bowls and casserole dishes on the stationary shelves too.

- Get an organizer for your coffee stuff, whether it be the sugar, cream, or whatever, and then, install small little hangers for your coffee mugs and have them within easy reach. It's simple but wonderful for your space.

- For the utensils, get one of those organizers for this. There are a variety of different types of organizers these days, and the best thing to do is to get one that fits everything, and from there, put your stuff back in. Don't try to just pile things up to wherever, but instead, have it neatly organized so this can be used.

- Water bottles can be stored with an organizer in cabinets, similar to how you store wine bottles. Having the water bottles on their sides does eliminate the chance they might fall and knock stuff over, and plus, you can always just grab and go with these and then move onto the next thing.

- Organize your stuff based on use, and if you have stuff that you use a lot, devote more room to it. If you're going to use it often, leave it out, otherwise, set it inside a drawer. You an even dote parts of your cabinet and counters to baking, putting everything in there so that you can add it all there, and easily attain it.

- Your pantry might already be neatly decluttered, but if you haven't organized it yet, you should consider using a lazy Susan for your species, sauces, and a door organizer for more storage if you need it. Make sure that your pantry is grouped ideally by alphabet, and keep the items you use the most right on hand for best results.

- Add hooks over your oven or stove, and from there, hang all of the utensils that you have on hand. Putting it all there gives you an idea of the areas of everything, and having these on a wood plank right above there keeps everything nicely in place, and you'll be happy to use these as well.

- For appliances, you can have them placed in a cabinet that's vertical, with shelving that you use to pull open. The best way to do this one is to add some labels, and if you have tall appliances, try to put them in smaller spaces, and neatly store them there. Remember to purge appliances that you don't need, selling as necessary.

- Keep stuff for kids pretty low, and if they do have school lunches, arrange it so that you can have it together and in a place for them to take at the beginning of the day is essential, and helpful.

Bathrooms

Bathrooms do require a certain level of organizing too. And here we'll highlight the best ways for you to organize your bathrooms so that you can actually find everything.

- If you haven't already, take a built-in shelving space, and put it under your sink. This is valuable storage space people don't need, and oftentimes, this can mean a difference between having room for what you need and what you don't have room for.

- Always have a small little space to keep everything off the counter. Try to keep only a few items there that you use. You should definitely try to make sure it looks nice too.

- Getting a foaming soap pump can enhance the room, and it doesn't require a lot of soap either to fill this. You can actually label it too with some free labels that you can find online and print out for even more fun.

- The inside of your cabinet doors is just as important as the inner cabinet themselves. You can use this for different hair styling products and the like. These over-the-door organizers are great for face towels and cleaning cloths.

- Get a toothbrush organizer, and try to put it under the cabinet. That way, it's easy to find, but also incredibly out of sight so that it doesn't look bad, and also is easy for you to grab when needed.

- Drawer dividers let you get the most out of your drawers. There are acrylic ones that work especially for the bathroom since it makes these light and airy, and it also lets you add the drawer liner for your own personal touch. Pretty nifty, aren't they?

- Get a caddy for each person in the home. Having a caddy for these items lets them have all of their hygiene products in one place. They can pull out the caddy, use it, and then put it back. That way, everything is there, and they don't forget things. Plus, it's very easy and quick to clean up. You can get small ones or big ones for this.

- If you don't already have a laundry bin, get one in your home. It doesn't need to be anything big, but having this is also good for any towels, other pieces of clothing that might've not made it to the room, so it helps to make laundry day a little easier on everyone.

- Try considering hanging towels from hooks instead of those towel bars. It's much easier to hang these forms a hook than a towel bar, it allows them to dry better, and it will definitely be much easier too. Towel bars are ideal for those who will actually use smaller towels, and this works. Getting a bunch of hooks for each person will help cut down on washing, and also help keep the place nice and clean.

- Finally, use clear acrylic containers and label everything on these containers. Labeling should be your best friend. You can use these on pretty much anything that you're buying or getting, and that will help you with your space.

Home Office

The home office is another place you should always have

ideas for organizing, and here, we'll highlight how to organize your home office.

- If you have a lot of cords, get those binder clips, and detangle the cables and USB cords. Clip these to the side of your desk, and then thread the metal part, so it's tangle free.

- The mason jar method is great for office supplies. Hot glue some mason jars together on the sides, and then have them on the desk. Use them on their sides then and put pens, pencils, staples, and small office supplies in them. Another great one to use in your crafting space as well.

- One way to store some of the items is a jelly jar for storage. Remove your shelf and place it upside down, and then screw, nail, or put the hot glue lid onto there, and keep the jars onto the shelf. This is a good way to keep things all neatly in place.

- If you don't already have a pegboard over your desk to help with your notes and papers, or even tape and scissors, consider having this in place.

- If you have old shutters, nail these to the wall. You can use this to hold some of the pending and paid bills that you have, or small pieces of paperwork, and you can use the top half as an inbox and the bottom half as an outbox. Little different, hey?

- If you have old shoeboxes, you can pin these together with clips in order to store different papers and books. You can also cover these with wrapping paper in order to be more decorative with the items.

- If you have an old magazine holder, paint these and cover them with some paper to match the decor, and from there, use them to hold various items, whether it be books, paperwork, or the like.

- If you have old cereal boxes, cover these with wrapping paper, and this will help with divided storage in your desk drawer. Consider using a Stanley knife in order to trim these to your own personal tastes.

Playing and Craft Rooms

The playroom and craft room are pretty good to also work in. Usually, these are chaotic, but with the right steps, and some of these cool ideas, you'll be able to add to this, and make your place even nicer as well.

- For pens and pencils, get a small cup, and put it on the desk in order to hold these.

- For different toys, get some small baskets, separate them by series or type, and then create a cubby system where you can put each of them inside the shelving to make this easier.

- Shoeboxes are great for dolls and doll parts, especially Barbie dolls or some doll clothing.

- For your crafting table, consider using a kitchen island to help with this, since it'll give you more room to work on.

- For leftover ribbon and items, get some old mason jars, and put the items into there.

- Organize all your ribbons based on color in drawers. You can wrap these around cardboard, and from there, you can set the drawers into space for you to hold yourself.

- If you have old magazine racks, you can add them here and use it to store not just your paper, but also your cardstock and craft foam.

- You can sort your buttons in different jars. You can get small little jars for the bigger buttons, and for the smaller ones, you want to use those three-inch spice jars for best results.

- If you have rubber stamps, line them up and stand them up. That way, when you need them, you just take them, and it doesn't affect the space, and it looks pretty cool!

Wardrobe, Closets and Clothes Room

Wardrobes and closets can be hard to organize, but here are a few ways for you to organize these spaces.

- Roll up your clothes and neatly tuck them in. It not only saves you some space, but also is great for making sure that you have a lot of space for your items, and it makes the drawers look neat and organized. Rolling clothes helps reducing ironing too!

- Get closet organizers and closet systems to put in place.

- A step stool in your closet will allow you to use the top shelves in the closet, and you'll be able to utilize that space instead of wasting it.

- If you need to use a double hang, do so, since it'll help with horizontal space within the closet.

- Consider over-the-door shoe racks to turn this place into the perfect locale for your accessories or shoes, or both of these things.

- Consider making sure that you keep the items you use the most nearby, and have the ones you don't use as much in different locales.

- Get some small shoeboxes to put the accessories such as different belts, gloves and the like to make it work.

- If needed, get a shoe rack, and use that to help with making sure that you get everything that you need, and to help organize all your shoes.

Storage

- Make sure all of your boxes are properly labeled with the item that they are, and when to use them.

- Make sure that you organize similar items together, so you're not wasting time.

- Check on this and make sure that you take inventory of the items that you have, so you know exactly what's up there.

- Depending on the space, you should make sure that you have some closed storage containers for items that you'll be putting away like holiday items or seasonal clothing.

- Plastic garment bags should be used for those clothing items that are there.

- Sometimes, if you have wrapping paper, you can get a small little storage container and hold them all in there.

- If you have the space, consider wall-mounted shelves and other furniture items if you don't have that already.

- Always label your items, so you know exactly where it is that you need to go for the items as well.

- If your storage space isn't an attic, consider having some wicker baskets in there and line them up vertically to help with putting different items away.

- Color coordinate containers based on seasons to help with easy access to storage and other items.

- Use clear containers for some of the items that you stock-pile that you need to see, such as canned goods, or bulk items that are around and causing trouble.

For most people, clearing out some of the excess clutter in their space is a wonderful way to ensure that you're getting the most out of every inch, to help you with getting the most out of your storage ideas, and out of the storage components that are already there

CHAPTER 10: TIPS FOR ORGANIZING YOUR STUFF

So how do you organize all your stuff? What are some good ways to organize everything so that it's possible to go through everything and make it easier for you? Well, read below to find out a few of the best organizing tips and tricks to help you with improving your home.

Old Trays and Bowls

While you may use all of your dishes, there are a few ways for you to use them for organization. One great way to organize a crafting or office space is to throw a non-slip mat into a drawer or box to keep them from moving, and then put the bowls in there. Then, put similar items into there. This is a great one if you have a lot of little things, and would prefer to use drawer space rather than jars and such.

Expose It All

If you aren't already exposing everything in your drawers when you open it, you'll realize that you're only wearing and rewarding the same few things. This can give you a reality of the amount of clothing that you have, and what you're working with. The solution is to fold the clothes in a way that's tight and small, and then store them into the drawers standing up rather than lying flat. That way, you'll see everything right there, and everything is there at a glance. This is kind of similar to how you see the books' spines on a bookshelf, and you'll realize that you either have a lot of clothes you never wear that you can toss, or you'll have a more creative and fun wardrobe that works for you as well.

Like with Like

The worst thing for you to do is to store things that aren't similar to one another, but if you have clothes and household items in multiple spaces, such as the closets, different baskets, or even storage bins, you'll probably forget what you own, and then you over shop for these items. You can from there keep grouped things in one drawer, and all of that is put together. Put items that are similar to one another in a desk, such as stamps, envelopes, pens, and pencils. From there, it's all in one singular location, and it reduces the instance of redundant and boring shopping, and it encourages you to go through and see what you have, weeding out stuff that won't work. When it's all consolidated, it's definitely better for you, and you're saving both money and storage space for items.

Keep Workspaces Clean

If this isn't already done, you need to keep your workspace clean and tidy. The reason for this one is that disorder will impact your long-term success and the fact that you don't have the right idea of where all your stuff is will negatively impact your ability to work and your filing systems. You should understand that our family photos and other small things will draw away our attention all the time. You should do a desk-sweep every now and then, and you should avoid all of the different distractions that are there, and it will help with the concentration and focus.

One of the best ways to think about this is to imagine that you have a hotel workspace, and remember, they keep this stuff clean, so make sure that you keep this nice and clean as well.

Streamlining Files

You need to start streamlining your filing system so that all of the paper and documents that you're using aren't sitting there. You should either use a three-tiered filing system, a file drawer for current projects that's close at hand, a second drawer for research material that you need, and then one for documents that are related to the projects that you've done for legal or personal reasons. The third drawer should be considered one that contains valuable documents, and one that you should make sure that you keep on hand for these types of reasons. It's worth considering, and this will help with making sure that you have the simplest and easiest means for this type of experience, and to make it so that you have all of your files on hand.

Try a Shelf Riser

This is a type of shelving that allows you to have double the amount of space in place for storage. This is a good one for those shorter and taller items, and personally, I like using this for a lot of my beauty products. For example, I use jars underneath these, and then the bottles that are up on top. This allows you to have a "spritz and go" sort of lifestyle, and it makes it easier for you to have everything in place that you need for your items.

Another part of this is to tier your shelves too. You will want to make sure that you have the more important items on the bottom, and then the less important ones on top. With this, aim to make sure that you see everything all at once so that if something is amiss, you can get it and then go.

Add a Towel Rack

Towel racks are great because they make organization better. Have you ever thought about adding a towel rack to the closet, such as a linen closet? This is something that a lot of people don't realize is a great one, but it isn't just for bathrooms. Having it over the door creates the out-of-sight storage space for the extra towels, throws, and tablecloths too. This is an excellent way to improve the way your towel rack goes, and it will also help with keeping all of your linens in place too.

Use Color!

If you're not already using colors for organization, you should start to do something about this. This is more than just coordinating your craft ribbons, paper, or clothes. If you're not using it for filing, you're missing out on a lot of the potential benefits that this has. This is great because it helps with adding a few extra ideas to this, and makes it more organized than ever before. Manilla filing folders might work, but if you have a ton of them, one of the best ways to make this work is to use colors for your sorting. For example, you can just glance at the colors and figure out exactly what it is that you need. This will, in turn, help with making sure that you have the right colors to sort everything and anything.

Toiletries on Hooks

Did you know that you can use this with your toiletries? This is pretty great. The best way to do this, however, is to get a second mounted shower curtain, but make sure that it's tension-mounted since it can get heavy. Next, you want to get some clips, such as C slips, and then put them on the shower curtain rail. This is best used close to the wall, opposite of the shower curtain, since it will have to hold a lot of various things. But you can pretty much hang any bottle of something up there that has a plastic tapered end to it. So lotions are great for this, and some body washes come in this form too.

Get Used to Hanging Things

Hanging your items not only looks good, but it also saves you a ton of shelving. We just discussed hanging your toiletries, and we've discussed hanging the office supplies, but one of the best things to hang is pots and pans.

Now, you can do this one of two ways. Either mount these against the wall on the side with some good hooks, or you can get something in the center that contains hooks, hang it up, and then hang all up here. With this, you should be careful about overloading, but try to hang the bigger pots and pans first, and then work towards the smaller items for best results and the best action possible. That way, you'll have everything neatly in the right place.

For most of us, hanging items is something that we should try to get used to, since this will help immensely with saving your storage space, and making it possible to put just about anything up as well.

Towel Bars Over Sink

Towel bars aren't just food for your towels, did you know that you could use this in your kitchen too? This has a similar sort of idea to the hanging idea that we discussed earlier, but a towel bar is great for pretty much any flat surface item. For example, measuring spoons, spices, mugs, or whatever you need, can sit nicely over the sink. The spice racks that they usually sell tend to get expensive, but a towel rack takes all of that out, making it easier, and much better for you to house everything into one specific place, making organizing better, and more possible. This is also good for those of us who are short, since it keeps everything neatly within reach.

Magazine Racks for Tools

We've discussed magazine racks for, of course, files and magazines. But did you know that they can be used for your tools as well for those of us with tool spaces, or crafting spaces that have some hot tools, or even hair products that get hot? You can take them and wind them up around the plug and cord (just be careful to make sure they have cooled down first), and from there, neatly put this in the rack I love this for hairstyling items such as curling irons, flat irons, and the like, and it's super easy and very cheap to use as well.

Get Used to Clear Items

Clear is probably the best color for pretty much any kitchen or personal storage item. That's because, if your kitchen has everything neatly seen, it'll be much easier to look at things. Most people don't realize that their kitchens could be organized better, but having some clear containers let you have a visible look at all of the food and items that you have. It will help with making sure that you have enough space that will work wonders for you, and the clear nature of these is good for you to utilize as well. Consider the clear nature of these canisters, since it'll help with improving the food space as well as quickly seeing what you need to buy.

Use Plastic Shower Pockets

Plastic shower pockets are great not just for shower items,

but they're also great for your car! I love using these because they can hold anything that you could need. Most parents are busy, and you should consider this option when storing items. From diaper bags to even a small snacks the kids can have, this is a great way to help you with improving your car space, and also makes it easier for going just about anywhere.

But, the cool thing about plastic shower pockets is that they can be used for many different spaces too. For example, crafting items can benefit from this, especially adhesives, and you can also use the hanging parts for a child's lunch or thermos. These are incredibly versatile and waterproof, and it's worth considering if you have a busy schedule, and you need something for on the go.

Organization can be hard to begin with, but here, you learned about a few powerful organization tools that'll help with improving your home, and different items with varying uses that are great for you to understand, and use in your space whenever you need to.

CHAPTER 11: DO LESS, LIVE MORE. THE SIMPLE AND MOST EFFECTIVE TO-DOS TO CREATE HABITS AND ROUTINES

Now, the big thing you should also look at is to consider using routines and different to-dos in your home when you're trying to do less and live more. There are a few things that you can use with regards to organization that'll change the game, and we'll discuss them here. They're important to mention, and here, you'll have everything you need on hand to create habits and some routines.

Make a To-Do List

If you're not doing this already, you should have a to-do list for yourself every single day. One of the problems we as humans face is that we're not always certain about what we should be doing next. Or worse, we worry that we're forgetting a very important item that we should've done the day before. And we have a feeling of struggle, hopelessness, and often, those thoughts don't fully go away. This is something that you should also consider if you're looking to keep the thoughts at bay. To do this, you should make a habit of writing down everything, including your short-term and your long-term goals. From there, you should create other to-do lists, separated based on tasks. Listing these out in steps where you need to work towards the goals will help with reclaiming the crisp, results-oriented mindset that you'll use to build and keep the momentum going.

If you finish a to-do, you cross it off. If you have certain days where you clean, then do that. If the goal is to organize the office by the end of the week, each day write down every single item that you need to do.

This might take a long time, but it's a very useful way to get everything that you need to be done, and it will help keep the momentum going, and keep you nice and strong. To-do lists should become your best friend, especially when organizing, and here, you've seen why most people are benefitting from this, and why they matter.

The "Mis En Place" System

This is a way for a lot of people, and it's more of a professional system that chefs have, but it's a wonderful system that works for many people. It translates to "put in place", which means that you want to gather everything that you need to do an action, such as cook a meal, and from there, clean the workspace and the utensils as you go along.

You can do this with just about anything, from using items

for crafting to even cleaning the bathroom. This is very good for keeping hygienic food practices in place too since it reduces the risk of bacteria contaminating foods, and that's something you don't want when you're in the foodservice business. This is a great one for a lot of people to just use in their homes, and it will help you prepare your items faster and more effectively.

Preparing your foods before you cook and clean as you go saves you a lot of time too. If you hate doing the dishes, this is a good way to reduce spending time doing those pesky dishes, and it will help with making cleaning and putting items away much faster as well.

Put It Back Where It Came From

This is something some parents struggle with teaching their kids, but this is a good way to make sure you don't have to spend hours and hours on end cleaning up your home.

The idea is, when you're done using something, you put it back where it came from. Whether it be toys, games, or absolutely anything. No matter what you use, you put it back where it came from when you're done. This is a way for you to put everything neatly back, and it will help keep you more organized daily. This will better your organization habits, and in turn, will help with improving your wellness, and happiness too. Having this in place will help with improving the daily activities of your space, and it will help you get into the habit of doing this.

I know how hard it can be to do it, but this is one of the best ways to keep your space properly organized and to make your home as versatile and comfortable as it can be.

Leave Items in the Same Spot

This ties into the previous point beforehand, but one of the best ways to get into the habit of making sure that you put it back where it came from, is to leave your keys, wallet, and other items in the same place every single day, and make sure that you have this in an obvious space. Hanging a little key rack in the entryway is a good way to do it. That way, you're never fumbling about wondering whether or not you misplaced these items. It also helps with making sure that you don't tear your entire place apart.

One of the best ways to do this is to get something that will hold the "smalls" as we call them. Entrance tables or a wall-mounted organizer are great for these types of things since they allow for you to store these items easily, and without too much trouble for either of you.

Use a Calendar

If possible, you should try incorporating a calendar into your home. Keep it in a space where you put down some of the different items that you have to go to or major events that you might not be ready for. This helps with an organized life, and you can make a shopping list, some to-dos, some errands, and the like that you need to have on hand.

If you want to have even more of a routine in life, sometimes carrying a small little pocket notebook is good for this. You can incorporate different errands and items you have to do, and some thoughts that might be there. It's very portable, great for users, and it will never need to be recharged like with some of the electronic planners. Upcoming events, notes on things, money spent, things of projects, and the like are great for this, and you can, with this as well, create the best experience that you can, and it's small, but effective for you to have a life that's incredibly organized, and effective as well. It will change the way you get through everything, and it will help with making sure that nothing is left undone.

Have Meal Plans

This is a simple way for people to stay on the ball with not just their home, but also their own body. Your meal plan is one of the easiest ways to stay organized .You can create a daily habit, and from here, update as necessary for you to use. Meal plans also help with creating habits since they allow for you to figure out what you need to make, if you have any items that you need, and cross out items that you don't need. It also puts a good plan of action on the place for you to be, and the time you need to cook these items and any containers that you need to have in place.

Meal plans are one of the simplest ways to ensure that you're getting everything done. Most don't realize it, but meal plans also help keep you on the right track too. You're less tempted to go out for meals, and you won't eat as many bad foods as a result of this. Understanding what it is that you need to make is very important for you to have in place, and in turn, it will help with ensuring that you're on the right track.

Put Together a Routine for Everyone

This isn't just for your kids or yourself, this is for everyone. The routine is everything that they need to do every single day. For kids, this includes laying out the clothes they need to get dressed, their lunches packed and prepared the day before, and where they need to be at what time. You can put together when people need to bathe and shower, and also when you should all be home and any of the events that need to be in place. This also works for chores too, and you should make sure everyone knows the plan and what they need to do for the week. Routines aren't just for you or the other person, but for everyone there, since this will in turn help with improving the way everything works, and the different types of tasks that are there for everyone.

Layout Clothing for the Following Day

This is something that everyone should start to do. Laying this out is the more efficient way of doing this sort of thing. This helps with keeping the critical time during the mornings when you're getting yourself and others ready as well. Laying out clothes the night before makes this easier, and it will save you a bunch of time when figuring this out.

This is something that you should do, not just with yourself, but also with your family, and it will help with this.

You should also make sure that the launch pad area, which is where you go before rushing out the door, is properly put together. You should have a coat rack there for any coats and items, and work bags, school bags, or gym bags, any ingredients for breakfast and lunch, any shoes or umbrellas needed, and anything else that you will want to make sure that you have in place before you begin. Having this routine in place will help keep you on automatic with this, improving your ability to handle everything.

Have an Exact Home for Everything

This final point is a little bit harder, but you should try to have an exact home for everything that you have. That way, when people ask you where something needs to go, you can rattle it off and tell them right away where it needs to go. Spices? Put them on the shelf! Toothbrushes? Have them in a spot under the sink. All of this is great because you'll be the person people will come to when they need to put items away, and it's important to make sure that you have an exact home for them to be in place, and you'll be able to, with all of this, have an exact place, and you'll realize that things are less hectic.

If you don't know where something should go, try to figure out a home for it right then and there. Don't let it sit around because then it'll cause further disorganization, and that's not good for everyone. Having the proper homes in place will ensure that you get everything neatly in its rightful home, and makes it so that you're able to, with the right ideas, create the easiest space to work with, and keep you organized.

Routines make organization better, and a routine allows you to do a whole lot less in life, and lets you do so much more too. If you haven't already put together a small routine or started to put a couple of great routines in place, then you'll want to do it now. The right routines will help with putting it all together, and you can, with these too, live a better, more organized life as a result of this process.

Try it, and you'll see the difference in this right away.

Simple habits and routines change the way you get your organization done, so remember that the next time you feel overwhelmed by the sheer span of your home. If you feel like you need assistance in making your home a simpler place to live, consider all of these tips to help make things easier.

PART 3: CLEAN YOUR HOME IN 15 MINUTES OR LESS

CHAPTER 12: WHAT YOU NEED TO KNOW BEFORE YOU BEGIN

When cleaning your home, there are a few things that make the job easier, and a few things that you should know before you start. It is important to have this mindset in mind before you begin, and in this chapter, we'll tell you what you need to understand before you begin, and why it's important to know exactly what you should before you start. That way, you won't get hung up on all of the stress of cleaning.

Stop Setting Impossible Expectations!

For many who don't clean a lot, they often think they have to have their home so spotless; someone will run their hands over things with a glove that's purely white and will not have a speck of dust on it.

Okay, but if you don't clean a lot, doesn't that seem like

excessive effort? People don't realize how stressful that can be for you, and how that can, without actually realizing the impossibility of that expectation, make you feel bad.

People don't realize that setting expectations and goals that aren't realistic won't help. If you only have 15 minutes to clean, you might not get a chance to deep clean one area. Spending an hour deep cleaning one space might be good for a once a month or every few months ordeal, but if you're doing weekly cleaning, you don't have to do that.

When you set up the goals that you need before you clean, you should make sure that it's possible to do. People don't realize that if you set the bar too high or the goal too lofty, you're not going to make it.

When setting these goals, make sure that you understand that while yes, it's wonderful to have high goals that you wish to achieve, also be realistic with the endeavors you wish to achieve with cleaning.

The last thing you want to do is expect to reach for the moon when you're stuck on the ground, and the same goes for cleaning. Don't go into this expecting giant things when you're tackling one area. Don't go in scrubbing it down so hard that your arm cramps. Just clean it, and just be honest with yourself about cleaning. It's a healthier mindset to go into and better for you.

The Number One Enemy: Perfectionism

Perfectionism is probably one of the worst enemies you'll have. That's because perfectionism is something that you should never try to achieve.

If you go into this thinking your home needs to be perfect, you'll fail. It doesn't need to be perfect; it needs to be cleaned.

That means that you clean the space, so it feels welcoming, better, and harmonious. Don't think that you have to just go into this with the idea that you're going to have a clean home, and everything will be okay.

If you're perfect, you'll start to spend way too much time trying to make sure everything is perfect, instead of getting the job done. I know people who obsess over perfectionism, who end up acting like they have to have the perfectly-cleaned home of their dreams. While you should always strive to have a gorgeous home that looks good and feels good, you should also be realistic with your ideas. Make sure that it's clean, but it's also not so clean that you hyper-focus on whether or not everything is perfectly cleaned or not. You should be honest with the way that it looks, and also don't get so hung up on cleaning that it affects you.

Perfectionism is what causes people to spend a bunch of time in one area when they could've just cleaned their whole darn house. It's a nightmare, it's never fun, and you need to be honest about it with the way cleaning is. Be forthright, and make sure that you don't get so focused on being perfect because it'll just make you feel like you're not getting anything done, and it can oftentimes make you feel as if you're going crazy every time you try to clean.

The 80/20 Rule

What is that exactly? The concept behind this is to get 80% of your result with only 20% of your effort. This is good because it prevents you from getting hung up on the effort that's put there. You'll definitely do a lot better if you're putting in less effort.

With cleaning, having a plan keeps you focused on the goal.

If you have a set cleaning schedule on who does it, when they do it, when it's time they do the job, and you're not sitting there worried about whether or not the job will get done. You're also not fighting through the concerns of getting it done, and you're not worrying about who is doing what.

It keeps your place less cluttered, and your brain less cluttered.

The best way to get a lot done is with minimal effort. This also involves balancing out everything that's there, and making sure that you're not doing everything all the time. You don't need to wash your windows every single month, nor do you have to clean the gutters every other month unless it's needed. Be flexible, but also be realistic about how you do it.

You should put that 20% of your effort into the places that need it. The kitchen and bathrooms are where the brunt goes, but for rooms and other living spaces, you might need to give them a dusting or two every now and then. You should understand that if you are focusing on the right stuff to focus on, you'll be better.

Your showers, toilets, and sinks all get dirtier than say, the bed in the guest room or maybe the pantry if you just use it for food storage. Be smart with where you clean your spaces and don't be afraid to do a little bit less.

Value Your Time

Just like with organizing and decluttering, your time is incredibly valuable. You shouldn't spend all that time trying to clean up one space. If you have one day off, and you're cleaning only for an hour, make it count. Don't get so hung up on the time you spend on something and don't obsess with doing so.

That's something most don't realize. Your time matters more than anything else, and you should always make sure that you work on improving your ability to get the job done. You need to understand that while it might not be perfect, it still is a good job.

That's a big part of cleaning your space. It's making sure you take the time to clean the space in a way that's effective and useful. Be honest with yourself, and with the time that you spend doing this, and if you feel like you're taking far too long on something, then stop doing it. You're not supposed to work on this for so long that you never get anything else done.

Your time is important, and if you're busy already, then you should work on trying to ensure that you use it in all the right spaces.

For some spaces, a yearly clean is fine. When it comes to washing your windows and shutters, do that once a year or so. That's a spring cleaning endeavor. But everything else has its own set time period, and if you know things will be easier for you.

You need to think of the time you spend cleaning as a finite period. Most people get so hung up on the aspects of cleaning that they don't realize it's only going to kill their drive. You need to, when you start cleaning up spaces, understand that you'll get more done with a plan.

That's why we encourage you to only clean stuff when you have a set schedule and plan, and from there, if you notice that something does have dirt on it, you clean it up. Don't get super into the nitty-gritty of what you need to clean, but just get the job done.

Plans are made for this reason. If you make a plan, you'll be much better off, and you won't get distracted by making sure everything is perfect.

Cleaning is similar to decluttering, since you're taking the time to clean out and take care of a space, and then after it's done, you move onto the next space. Value how your space is handled by looking at each of the areas, and plan accordingly.

CHAPTER 13: THE BEST TOOLS FOR CLEANING!

Now that we've gone over the importance of getting the job done, let's talk about how to clean. What are the best tools for cleaning? What will get the job done quickly and effectively? Read below to find out.

Microfiber Cloths

When you clean a space, microfiber cloths will be your best friend. Lots of people think you need a feather duster or a sponge, but a microfiber cloth will hold on to the dust quickly and easily. Once it's rinsed off, it will be able to use it easily. Plus, the dust doesn't randomly fly away with microfiber cloths.

They're great for cleaning just about anything, from tiles to glass, and it's even good for pet hair off your clothes. One way I like to do it is to have one color to use within the bathrooms, another one for the kitchen, and a third for all of the other areas.

Gone are the day of using those ugly, cumbersome dusters, but instead, you can benefit from this with a simple microfiber cloth. That way, your space is cleaner, and it takes much less time to get the job done.

Vacuums

Vacuums are good for hardwood flooring and of course, carpet. Carpets need this, so a high-quality vacuum will go a long way. I like the kind with a hose on it since you can get it in all of those corners. You can use a hand vac to remove pet hair off the upholstery, freshen up mattresses, and is good for both interior and exterior areas. Even if you don't use a vacuum on a hardwood floor, I encourage you to get one of those stick and hand vacuums.

Stick and hand vacuums also work amazingly in the kitchen since they can get into those little corners far better than a broom and dustpan do. Along with that, there is also the fact that every time you use a broom and dustpan, there's that tiny little line left behind. A vacuum eliminates all of that.

Entrance mats can even be benefitted from with a small vacuum. Once a week, you can give the entrance mat one quick little vacuum over, and it cuts down on the dirt you track inside as well.

This is great if you're someone who wants everything all in one place, and this is indeed how you do that.

Dusting Extensions

If you have high ceilings and you're someone that suffers from indoor allergens, you'll want to get a duster to go up there. But the problem is most people are either too short to reach this or even if they aren't, they need a step stool to get to even the highest chandeliers and light fixtures. Kitchen cupboards do benefit from this too since they are usually too high for the average person. Extension dusters are wonderful, and they offer you a chance to ensure that you have the right length on this, and the perfect dusting experience.

Spray Bottles Along with Homemade Cleaners

Are you tired of having to spend a lot of money on cleaners? Unless you require bleach, you can make spray bottles and fill them up with water, lemon essential oil, and soap to create a nice and beautiful smelling home cleaning product. You might want to refrain from the essential oil if you have pets, but if you want to make your job easy, you can put the soap and water into a spray bottle, and then use it.

If you want to use spray bottles as well, you can just fill them with water to get the article of clothing ready to be ironed, or even used to train your pets to get away from areas where they don't need to be.

This is a great thing to have, and you can have different cleaners in each of these, and it's wonderful to use if you feel like you're someone that has a lot of cleaning to do, but you don't always want twenty different cleaners.

Scrubbing Sponges

SOS pads and scrubbing sponges are ideal for those tough areas or those areas covered in grease like your oven or sink. These are really tough, they're wiry and take a long time to fully break down, but they are wonderful if you're someone who needs something that gets all of those troublesome areas.

If you have areas with dirt that accumulates, this is how you handle that, since they're ultimately easier to clean if you spend time using these rather than other options that you have. Even just a good scrubbing sponge makes getting grime off the tough locations easier.

Steam Mop

This is a great one to get the grout and the tile cleaned at the same time. If you have washable pads for this too, it works too. Shower stalls that are awkward to clean do benefit from this too, and they make sure that the walls are clean. Pretty much almost any surface that's glass can benefit from this, and you can even get some baseboards and facades with this type of cleaner, and it can benefit you immensely as well.

White Cleaning Cloths

White cleaning cloths are probably some of the best for removing any clothing and carpet stains. That's because, colored fabrics will transfer the dyes and from there, expand the problem to make it worse. White cleaning cloths are also super cheap.

These washcloths aren't just good for those who want to clean their home, they're wonderful for removing makeup and other dirt that's there. You can use them to clean up different areas. They can even be used with pet bedding or filling for throw pillows. They're incredibly versatile and they work wonders for you.

Broom and Dustpan

All right, so if you do have hardwood floors, you probably don't want a super huge vacuum. If you're willing to make the job easier for you and get those tough areas that the vacuum can't, such as behind your toilet and the like, then get yourself a broom and dustpan. You can use this along with the vacuum to help clean up everything and make it look better and it's easier for you to do as well. There is a lot that you can do with this, and a lot of amazing benefits that you can do to ensure that you have the right cleaning experience for yourself.

Spin Mop

If you're someone who wants a good mop that's a little more old-fashioned, and you're not really feeling the steam mop or the microfiber mop system, then you should just get a spin mop. These are more of the old-fashioned mop systems, and this one is a spinner that operates with a pedal, so it controls the flow of the water as well. It's very easy to use. On Amazon, there's a ton of wonderful options, and they are good pieces of cleaning equipment.

Wood Cleaner

The problem with some wood finishes is that the wood tends to suffer if there is water applied to it. The solution to that is a wood cleaner. This is good for wooden surfaces and wooden finishes. And it is very easy to use and highly effective as well. Wood cleaners also help eliminate streaks and spots, and they are incredibly useful. These are good for those troublesome kitchen cabinets that tend to have a lot of work added to them, and for those areas that usually require you to use specialty cleaners on them.

Gripping Brush

What, you don't like to use the same sponges for toilets as you would for maybe those troublesome corners? These types of brushes come with that handy little grip added to them that make the job easy, and it also works to make the job a lot of fun. If you're someone that hates dealing with the annoyance of brushes that don't sit right, or maybe you can't reach those corners very well, then you may want to get this one. It also saves you a lot of time on deodorizing and cleaning, as well.

This is good for the kitchen, especially those awkward

corners where the drains are, and also those areas that require a little bit more cleaning to them, and it is really helpful for you. They're usually forma cleaners with bristled edges, which means they're very easy to use, and they'll get the job done right away.

Stainless Steel Cleaner

Stainless steel cleaners are the last thing that you need, especially if you have stainless steel items. This is mostly because you will need to clean these in a specific way, but you should consider buying one of these, since it makes the job a little easier on everyone. It reduces the abrasiveness that other cleaners would have, keeping your appliances nice and useful.

And there you have it, all of the tools that you need to ensure that you get the most out of this that you can, and also to help you clean your home readily and easily.

CHAPTER 14: CLEANING TIPS FOR EACH AREA OF THE HOUSE

While you may not clean every area of the house right off the bat, here is a room-by-room guide to cleaning every single area, and what you should minimally do to have a clean space.

While some people might get into the nuances of cleaning, that doesn't mean that you have to be the same way. These are just the minimal options, and it might be beneficial if you're someone that doesn't want to spend copious amounts of time cleaning your stuff.

The Living Room

The living room is your priority, and it's incredibly easy to clean. Below are some of the easy things to do and things that will help with cleaning your living room

- Dust all of the lampshades or use a lint roller to clean them off.

- Use a lint roller to clean off the upholstery too, and make sure the blinds are lightly cleaned off too.

- Wash any of the throws and fluff your pillows as needed.

- Clean off anything that shouldn't be on the sofa with a hand vacuum or using your hands.

- Vacuum the areas under the couches too, since stuff loves to accumulate.

- Polish down your furniture with a wood cleaner.

- Use a microfiber cloth on some of the different electronics there. However, do not use a water-based cleaner but instead, wipe them down.

- Dust any knickknacks with a hand duster or cleaner.

- Always go into this from top to bottom, and make sure that you don't vacuum everything first, but instead, go it at the end.

- Wipe down your ceiling fan since it's simple and prevents all of the dust and other mites from getting around.

- Have your welcome mat shaken outside as needed, so you don't track dust in.

- Fold all blankets and throw them neatly in a basket or corner.

Bedrooms

For the bedroom, it's very simple to clean up too, and there are a few ways for you to clean this up quickly, and effectively.

• For ceiling fans, you can use a duster or sponge to do this easily, or you can get an old pillowcase and clean up your fans and light fixtures, and make sure that when you're done, put them off to the side away from the bed.

• Clean down any mirrors with water and a microfiber cloth.

• Wipe down all surfaces in the area and clean off anything on the nightstands or dressers.

• Take blankets and put them neatly on the bed. If you can, make your bed as well.

• Wipe down your windows with a window cleaner too.

• Use a lint roller again to help clean the curtains, and make sure that you don't track any of that onto any clean bedding.

• Vacuum the floors or sweep them down, making sure to get all corners.

The Kitchen

The kitchen is probably going to be your messiest locale. It's the messiest for most people, but here we'll tell you some of the best ways to clean it down, and some ways to make it easier for you.

• Start at your sink and take care of dirty dishes.Get rid of any dishes that need to be cleaned and put them away as soon as possible.. We don't always clean it, but instead, clear it and clean any dirty dishes.

• Wipe down the fridge with a microfiber cloth or even a scrubbing sponge since it might need it. The curved handle might be helpful here too to get those tight spaces.

• Spray down the surfaces and the stovetop, working from top to bottom, and then, let the cleaner sit. Don't scrub it right away, but instead wait for it to do its thing before you come back.

• Clean down any top surfaces that you can first, and get any of the shelves on top, the light fixtures, and your cabinets too, including the top of the fridge, but do this quickly.

• Clean your microwave and do so by setting a sponge that's wet into there and literally "cook" the sponge for a few minutes. Take a warm rag and dip it in some water and wipe down the doors and sides of the area around the kitchen, or even around the microwave sides... When the sponge is cooled down, wipe both the outside and the inside of the microwave for best results.

• For the stovetop, you should get some baking soda for the stubborn stains. Granite countertops need a specific cleaner and so do stainless steel surfaces, so it's important to make sure that you clean these all down effectively.

• Clean down the vertical surfaces after the horizontal ones, and make sure you get the sides and the handles.

• When you finish, wipe down the sink, and make sure you use an abrasive for the tough stains. When finished, toss the cloth and other items, empty trash, and vacuum or sweep the surface.

Bathroom

The bathroom is going to be your grossest location probably, but it's one of those places that, once it's cleaned up, it looks a lot better. A bathroom that's left unkempt will drive anyone crazy.

• For the shower, you start from the top, and you use a mop to clean it going down or use a scrubbing brush.

• You can also get a grocery bag and fill it with white vinegar, and from there, place it on the showerhead. Remove and rinse.

• Wash your linens and curtains with regular detergent, along with the towels to get rid of mildew on it.

• Clean down any dingy mildew and such with a grout brush and make sure that you get all of the areas since grout is porous, and it does cause bacterial growth.

• For your tiles, make sure that you use an all-purpose

cleaner on all of these, and let it sit and mix before you wipe it down.

• Use baking soda on your toilet and make sure that you let it sit for a bit and then brush.

• For bad toilet spots, what you do is get a pumice that's damp and abrasive enough to remove all of the stains that are caused by the mineral deposits on lime, but also gentle enough not to damage the surface.

• Only use an outlet brush after you've worked on getting all of the other stains off of this.

• White vinegar and baking soda poured down your drain and flushed with hot water will keep all the pipes and drainage nice and clean.

• Use disinfecting wipes to reduce the bacteria in this area since the cloths might transfer the germs from the toilet to the sink.

• Use floss on the faucet, and that's because it gets those grimy spaces between the faucet and your taps as well, and it also cleans the sink easily.

• Finally make sure to de-germ your bathroom vent, and flip it on, remove the cover, and then soak it with a water dish and soap, and from here, wipe it down with a cloth.

• You can also use a paintbrush to get the insides and the nitty-gritty of your bathroom's fan.

• For the floor, either clean it down with a sponge or with a mop and a bucket with hot water.

The Home Office

The home office is probably the one location that you don't spend a lot of time working on, but it's very important to ensure that you have a clean home office too. Here, we'll tell you how to clean down your home office, so it looks spick and span.

• Dust down all the bookshelves, and use a soft-bristle paint-brush to help clean the bindings of books.

• Use an electrostatic dust mop on the storage containers to wipe them down and keep them clean.

• Wipe down your desk surface from top to bottom with a microfiber cloth, picking up anything as you go along the way to dust.

• When cleaning the computer, only use a microfiber cloth, and from there, work from top to bottom, the CPU, and the keyboard with a microfiber cloth, and then use this cloth to wipe down the printer fax machine, and electronics.

• Wipe down the filing cabinets, tables, and other items in your office with a microfiber cloth, from top to bottom. Do all of these but the desk chair.

• For the desk chair, first you vacuum this directly with the brush attachment, and spot treat any of the stains and spills that are seen with a cleaner and cloth.

• Use the cloth to wipe down from top to bottom, and if you notice that the cloth isn't doing enough for it, use a toothbrush, and wipe down the wheels with a toothbrush to scrub necessary spots.

• Disinfect the telephone and remote controls with disinfecting wipes and get all the areas where you use them.

• Use a duster and microfiber cloth to get the light fixtures, and for a fan, wash the fan with a pillowcase to remove the dust.

• Clean your blinds and curtains by using a vacuum on a lower setting with the brush attachment.

• Finally, vacuum everything where you have it, and make sure that you get all of the different areas with the vacuum, moving furniture as needed to clean underneath items.

Craft and Play Rooms

For craft and playrooms, it can get a little chaotic in there. In this, we'll discuss what you should do with all of that stuff in your craft room so you can easily clean it up.

• Go through your supplies, and get rid of any dried paints, primers, mediums, and resins, and make sure that you see if your paints are usable.

• Take all of the crafting items and put them in their spaces.

• Clean up any scrap papers and such. You can use them for

other things such as confetti, but if it's not something you need in the immediate future, it's better to toss.

• Wipe down all of the shelves with items, cleaning down any boxes and such with a microfiber cloth.

• If you have a sewing machine, clean it and the foot pedal down with a microfiber cloth.

• For any stains and spots on the floor, scrub them off with a sponge or SOS pad if it's really bad.

• For any toys that aren't put away or any dirty toy sets, get a microfiber cloth and start to wipe all this down.

• When you finish up, you can also sweep the floor, and use a mop whenever you can to ensure that you get the most out of your cleaning experience.

• For crafting projects, make sure the right items are in the right place and wipe down.

• Clean down all shelving too with a microfiber cloth.

• You can vacuum or sweep down the floors if you feel like a vacuum would limit your ability to clean up the space.

Cleaning Your Closets

What they don' tell you, is that closets can reek of dust, since it accumulates a lot of dust and grime. Here are some hacks to clean your closets and storage spaces, so they stay nice and clean.

• For closets with actual items in there that you use every day, make sure to take stuff off the top shelf, wipe it down, and then put it back.

• For items that are hanging, go over them with a microfiber cloth.

• Wipe the base of each shelf in a closet since they might get dirty.

• Use a microfiber cloth to wipe down shoes and other items since yes, dust does accumulate on those.

• For any boxes and storage containers, wipe these down as well with a microfiber cloth.

• If you have any grime on the floor, either sweep it, use a mop on it, or a vacuum.

• You can also clean the sides of the hangers with a microfiber cloth, since it will help with cleaning the place down.

• If you're using the organization method where you check to see if you've worn something by turning it around, make sure to check this each time you go into the closet, and if you see unworn stuff, get rid of it.

• Wash any area rugs that you have in there, or any spaces where you leave shoes on since this can attract dirt and grime.

Storage Areas

Storage areas usually don't have to be cleaned all that much, but it depends on whether you go in there a lot. Here, we'll give you a few hacks for cleaning down your storage space, so it looks better and feels nicer.

• Rotate your content here too, so that if something is touched or untouched, you will know, and it's not just sitting there.

• Start with the top, and take inventory of everything that you have in there, and make sure you see stuff that you are using and are organized.

• With a microfiber cloth, you want to go down from the top over each of these areas, and from there, wipe down all the boxes, and excess dirt and other items.

• For boxes that have glitter on it, such as those with Christmas decorations, wipe down all the glitter into a pile.

• Once that's all done, clean any light fixtures there too.

• After that, get a vacuum and also work on cleaning up any of the excess dirt and grime.

With the storage spaces such as your garage, it's usually good to go up and down with a microfiber cloth. As a note too, you don't need to worry about this being a big part of your cleaning routine, unless, of course, you are going to be using the space a lot. But, usually just going through this once every few months is your best bet, since it isn't a space with a lot of usage.

Cleaning your home and storage space is incredibly important, and in this chapter, we discussed how you can do it with each area, in a way that will benefit you, and in a way, where you're getting the job done easily and without too much trouble.

CHAPTER 15: THE 15-MINUTE CLEANING STRATEGY — HOW TO CLEAN YOUR HOME IN JUST 15 MINUTES!

Alright, when we say 15-minute cleaning, we mean a quick, 15-minute cleanup of the home. While this type of cleaning isn't ideal for the tough-to-reach spaces in your home, it's really important for those looking to quickly take care of cleaning since it isn't fun. Here, we'll go over how you can do it, almost as if you're hustling to get the place spruced up for guests as they come over. It might seem like a lot of work, but it's possible, and here, we'll highlight just how you can clean your home in a mere 15 minutes, and the best way to go about doing this.

If you have areas that need a deeper clean, you'll want to make sure that you have a little bit more time for cleaning. But if you don't have the time, or the desire, to clean it quickly and want to hit everything in one fell swoop, this is how.

As a note too, the more you clean, the better it is to maintain and the easier it is. So while the first time it might take forever if you keep up with the cleaning schedule, over time you'll do even better, and you'll be happy that you did this. So what are you waiting for? It's time to clean like crazy!

You can do the entire place in one fell swoop, or you can work every single day for 15 minutes clean a space. We'll tell you how to clean a home with just 15 minutes of work, and how you can set a schedule.

Specific Room Focus

The big thing to remember is to work on the big rooms, which are the bathrooms, the kitchen, and the gathering space. If you're cleaning quickly for company, you can literally just focus on these.

For the living room, you should minimally stash clutter away, work on fluffing and folding blankets, cleaning and vacuuming the floor, and also dusting down anything that has obvious dust on it and wiping down the TV.

For the kitchen, think of the hot items such as the oven and stove, the sink, and the front and sides of the fridge. Wipe these down with a microfiber cloth, or also some cleaner, and from there, wipe down the spaces.

You want to focus on the bathroom but focus primarily on the toilet and sink. Give these a nice wipe down, and from there, also consider what the shower looks like too. If you're pressed for time, you don't clean it. You should as well look at cleaning the kitchen and the den, and sweeping it down, rather than vacuuming it cause that takes a little bit more time and more equipment.

The focus should be to wipe down the surfaces that you have, and make sure that they are nicely cleaned off. You should also have dust clothes to get rid of the dust that's there, and it would best be used in areas where people may not know. The same goes for disinfectant wipes so that you can wipe these down on surfaces of the bathroom, and of course, on the kitchen counter.

But what if you're someone who wants a more standard cleaning schedule, where you don't have to hustle and put everything away in just 15 minutes? Wouldn't this be easier? Of course, it is! You can do it, and here, we'll tell you how to put together the simple cleaning schedule that will help you.

The 15 Minutes a Day Cleaning Schedule

This type of schedule focuses less on just preparing the home and hoping to so that nobody sees any faults, and more on doing a little bit each day. While yes, you might notice that you have a messy bathroom or bedroom, you can use this type of schedule to help you get the most out of this.

How do you do it? Well, we'll tell you each day what you should do and what will be best. This is a good strategy to employ, however, after you've done the cleaning already and want to maintain it. This is better for maintenance rather than going down and cleaning everything.

For Monday, you vacuum, and you vacuum the entire house completely. Vacuum the rooms, sometimes do your vents and curtains and the crevices of windows. If your home is really big, it might take a little more time, but 15 minutes should suffice. Some people use a robot vacuum to get all the surfaces clean for an easier time. If you want to do it another way, literally sweep down the hardwood surfaces, and then vacuum at the end if you have hardwood floors throughout your house.

Tuesday is dust day, and this should take about 15 minutes, but this also depends on the knickknacks you have. You may need to wipe down the furniture as well with the furniture polish that you have too.

On Wednesdays, you have the bathroom. This might be your only bathroom, or it could be your main bathroom. But what you want to do is you should clean down the toilet, the counters, the mirror, the tub, the shower, and of course, your floors. In general, the total time for the bathroom should be around 15 minutes or so.

On Thursdays, you can do this again, or alternatively, if you don't have another bathroom, but you have a playroom and craft room, you clean these down, simply by picking up some of the items that you have and making sure everything is kept nice and tidy. This again should only take 15 minutes, and usually, it's just cleaning anything extra that you have on the ground.

The kitchen is what you do on Fridays, where you clean down the countertops and surfaces with the product, and you also wipe down the fridge and the tops of surfaces. This is something that again, should take you no more than about 15 minutes.

Now Sunday, you have two options. Either you don't do a darn thing, or you do small projects. That again is dependent on how your home is looking. If you have cleaning projects you've been holding off doing, such as the storage rooms and your closets, you do them at this time. This is something simple and yet very effective.

When you look at this, you might wonder if I'm joking or something. After all, it's super simple, right? Well that's the thing, it doesn't need to be some in-depth cleaning once you have it clean. People think cleaning should only be done when it's dirty, but that really isn't the case.

Cleaning is done when it is scheduled to be done, or if there is a mess that should be picked up right away. The idea behind it is if you do clean this, you immediately get it out of your life, out of your hair, and it's all taken care of. You should put all the times away in a basket, and sort out the mail for anything that comes in. Throw out all junk, and from there, make sure that everything is picked up.

This might seem very simple to the average person. But,

here's the thing, with this type of system, it's a maintaining step. You're not working towards perfections.

While in the last chapter we gave some awesome cleaning hacks, you've got to understand that it's not necessary to do it like this. Not at all. In fact, I don't recommend you do it all like this, but instead, you should wipe it all down. You need to look at the space and envision how you want to do this.

You have to work from top to bottom as well. It saves you time and effort when cleaning up the different spaces, and it's pretty easy.

Skipping?

This is something I honestly only recommend if you are desperate and don't have time for it. For those who parents are expecting, who have appointments, or those dealing with potty training, a kid crying all day, or whatever, you should skip it only if it's unable to be done. While it won't hurt your house if it isn't done in a specific week, you don't want to create a habit. This does make a difference though, especially if you look at it this way.

The idea behind the 15 minutes of cleaning a day isn't to force you to have to do it like it's a chore, even though it technically is a chore, it's important to realize that if you treat it like this, it takes far less time, and far less effort to get it done. It makes it so simple, and also very effective for you too. It's a fun way for you to easily create and clean your home, offering you the best and simplest experience for you to attain.

Cleaning your home in just 15 minutes a day is utterly possible and doable, and you'll realize that, once it's all taken care of, and you've fully cleaned it, you'll be happier than ever before, and you'll be able to attain it all.

PART 4: HAVE FUN!

CHAPTER 16: HOW TO GET THE FAMILY TO WORK TOGETHER

You will need assistance with this one. That's because getting your family to clean isn't always the easiest thing, but it is completely possible. In this chapter, we'll discuss how to get everyone involved in cleaning and how you can do it too.

Do or Delegate — How This Gets Everyone to Cooperate

This is a concept that's important to utilize when you're trying to get everyone to work together.

The idea is that either you say you're going to do it, or you delegate it to other people. This can be anything from washing the dishes to even dusting the knickknacks on the shelf. You either do this, or you delegate the task to others.

There is power in numbers, and there's a lot of benefits to be had if you spend time giving other people different tasks rather than doing it yourself. For example, do you want to spend all your time vacuuming all the floors and areas, or would you rather delegate it to another person in the house?

The general idea you should follow is that if it's something that can be done by someone to a satisfactory result, then you should delegate it. If you know the other person won't screw it up, then you should delegate it.

If it's a specialized task, then you should do it. That's because you're kind of the "expert" in that case, which means that you're the one who knows what to do in this case, and you should make sure that you do the job how you want it to be done.

But, if you think you can easily get the same results from someone else, delegate it.

There's a concept in making lives less stressful in the office, where you should try to delegate at least 2/3 of the tasks to others. While some stuff is usually best done by yourself, for these chores, if you get others involved, it saves you so much time.

For example, if you spend an hour cleaning every day, and you've got 4 people in the house, have them each take a quarter of the work. That brings your cleaning down to 15 minutes.

Everyone can get involved in this. And the best way to do this is to sit down with everyone in the home and get an agreement between all parties on what it is that you need done, and what they're willing to help you with. If you know what that is then you'll be good to go.

Delegating tasks is so important for people who are looking to get the most that they can out of the time that they spend cleaning. You can save yourself so much time if you do this, and it saves a ton of headaches and hardships, so if you can, always work to delegate all the tasks at hand, and make it so that you're able to, without fail, make the job of cleaning your home and making the space more functional for everyone.

You can start using this today by going through a list of the tasks at hand, and rattle off who does what. You'll then have everyone on the same page of what exactly needs to be done, saving you a lot of headaches and annoyance too.

How to Get Kids to Get Involved in Cleaning

For many parents, this can be the hardest step. Children are incredibly helpful with cleaning and decluttering the home, but there are two concerns most parents have when they try to get their kids to help.

The first of these is what they can do. What can children do in this case? It does ultimately depend on what their capabilities are, but children are great for cleaning assistance. You'll be amazed by the results this will get, and the fun that's there.

Now some chores are better for kids than others. For example, if you're looking to get younger kids involved, maybe have them get used to putting their toys away, making their bed, or picking their stuffed animals up off the floor.

Slightly older kids can help with dusting some areas, or even just using the sponge on surfaces that are closer to their height to help get the lower areas.

Some older kids can handle more involved chores. For example, if you have vacuuming, sweeping, or even doing laundry, they can help with that and make the job easier.

However, do be fair to your kids. Give them a chore list of things they should do. Don't force them to clean the whole house like some parents, but instead, be fair with it. Give the same amount of chores to each of the kids, and get incentives in place to make them do this. For example, if you know they like an allowance, give them an allowance each week for doing the job. If they do the chores for X amount of weeks, they can get some ice cream or another treat. It's a wonderful way to get everybody involved, and it's a fun way to make the job even better and more doable for everybody that's doing it.

For a lot of people, there are a lot of benefits to be had from this, so definitely consider all of these different things kids can do so that they can help with the chores. You should make sure they're doing stuff that's within the age range and provide reasons and incentives for doing things too.

Treat This like a Game!

It is a game in a sense, and it's important to realize that if you treat it like this, you'll be much happier off. Cleaning isn't fun, decluttering isn't fun, and organizing can be so boring, but sometimes, treating this like a game is something that most people end up doing. If you do end up treating stuff as a game, you'll be so much happier.

For example, try treating putting away dishes as a race to see how quickly you can get it done. For children, you could say that the one who puts their toys away the fastest gets an extra treat, or maybe they get to choose the next movie for family movie night. You can even make a game up where an evil monster is going to come in 15 minutes, and they need to put their toys away and clean up the bedroom fast! You can even tell them as well that they're competing against their siblings to see who will get the job done quickest.

No matter what you do, where you go with this, and how you do it, you should try making a game out of it.

Games help get kids excited. It's a little less like cleaning and a little more like a fun game that can certainly make things easier. If you notice that your children aren't all that interested in doing this, it can give them a reason to. A lot of people don't realize how helpful a game can be with this, since it can ultimately make it possible for you to deal with a lot of the chores easier.

If you notice your kids are reluctant to clean up, then you should consider potentially doing this, since it gets everyone on the right track, and helps push forth new games to keep them stimulated, since kids will love it if there is a possible game in the fray here.

Games are fun, and they're good for kids, since they can make dealing with the job a lot better.

Races are usually the best kinds of games in this sense since most people who do races tend to get the kids to all work together. They can do races against the other siblings, or even against the whole house. All while making it a decent experience for them too.

Lots of parents get a lot of great benefits from this, and you should consider this type of thing if you want your kids to all work together, and to make it easier for everyone as well.

For some parents as well, making it a game makes it easier for them. It keeps them motivated, and it can be a way to try and better this type of experience too. For most parents, it can make things easier for them to accomplish the tasks, and even those who aren't parents and are just trying to make their home nicer, it can improve on this markedly.

There are many different ways to make cleaning possible, and I encourage you to get everybody involved. That way, people are contributing to the household, so you're not doing everything, and you also end up with a cleaner, better home than ever before.

CHAPTER 17: HOW TO STAY MOTIVATED

Let's face it: cleaning is super boring, and not always the most fun thing. If you have a big home, this is even harder to accomplish. You need to learn how to stay motivated, though, to get more done and to feel happy.

For larger spaces, this is very important, especially since it can take a long time. If you have hoarder tendencies, this is a great way to get the job done, and you'll be really happy with the efforts over time. Staying motivated, however, can be a struggle, because it can be a lot of work. Most people don't realize how annoying it can be, and how it can be for some people. But, in this chapter, we'll give you some good motivational tips to keep in mind, and efforts to apply so that you can stay on track, and stay happy with the results that you get from this. Most don't realize how important this is, and how things will change with the right motivation and the right ideas to have.

You Need That Motivation, so Stay Inspired!

Motivation comes in so many forms. Whether it be the idea of a fully organized home, having something that looks like something out of a Better Homes and Gardens catalog, or whatever, having the correct motivation is something we all can benefit from.

Motivation is something you can use even in the worst of times, in the harshest of moments, and it can change the way you do things.

Most people don't even realize that this is so important for the majority of us, and it's something that a lot don't realize will help us get through the worst to get the job done.

For example, if you know the best motivation for yourself is you will be able to spend less time looking for items, then this might be a good thing for you.

If you know your motivation is to have less clutter on the floor, then use that as your drive. If you have a dream home that you'd love to emulate, but it requires you to clean up the space, then do that. The biggest thing to remember is whatever you choose, you need to have the motivation in place.

With anything in life, motivation is the reason why stuff gets done. It's the reason why you get what you want, and why things work so well for you and work out swimmingly. If you don't have that, you can say goodbye to getting the job done.

And one way to also do this is to make a goals list. You can write down both the main goals and sub-goals that you will want to keep in mind. You can even make a timetable of all the different stuff you want to get done, and how long it will take to do all this. That way, you'll have an idea of what exactly it is that you need to do to achieve the results that you want.

What most don't realize is that if you have goals and you have a game plan, you'll have a great time. That's because, if you have a set idea of how you want to achieve every-thing, you can always come back to this.

Sometimes, even keeping motivational quotes around to look at every so often helps too. While it might seem weird to do this for cleaning a house, it's useful and helpful, and it will be beneficial for you as well when you need that extra bit of motivation.

Sometimes, if you talk to other people who are doing similar things, it helps a lot. Maybe you can talk to other friends or even family members, and all of you make a game out of this. The person who cleans their house up the best and the fastest wins. This can be great for some people, and it can give you a reason to do it, even on those days that you don't want to.

You can also try the motivation of big parties. Having a big party, for example at a certain time, will help you stay motivated too since this big party can account for a lot of the different parts of life, and also account for all the things you want to have accomplished. If you do have a big party set for a certain period of time, you can clean up the house, and from there, try to declutter and organize your space, and from there when it's time for guests to arrive, you're not shoving stuff in the closet, but instead, you're showing everyone your wonderful, beautiful abode.

Whatever your reason is or isn't, have some motivation there, and it's very important to understand that the right motivation will help immensely. It will change the way you handle life and the way things go. By having the correct motivation in place, you'll be much better off, and it can help you with improving your wellness too.

How You Can Stay Inspired

How do you stay inspired in the face of so much work? How do you stay positive throughout all this?

Well, there's a lot that you can do to accomplish this. For example, you need to sit down and think about what inspires you. Is it the idea that you'll be able to find everything quickly and effectively? Or is it the fact that you also have a plan that works and makes sense for you to do? Whatever it is, you should look at the inspiration you want to have, and what will get you excited and happy.

It doesn't have to be something huge. It can be something

small, but that little nugget of inspiration will keep you nice and on track, and you'll be ready to make it work.

I personally like to look at different areas for inspiration. Some of the different areas where you'll feel inspired include the following:

• Magazines

• Other people's homes and spaces

• The different pictures online

• Brainstorm ideas on how having a clean space inspires you

• Different benefits of having a clean home, and how it can benefit you.

All of these different ways will help you improve your home and the space that you have. What many of us don't realize, is that if we don't take the time to look for the inspiration that we want to have when you get the job done, it can make decluttering almost like a chore.

Sometimes, also looking at just how far you've come will help too. I remember when I started to clean my space, I felt a bit bogged down by the way things were going. I started to, with the cleaning that I did, imagine all of the progress that was happening in my space, and everything that was going on. I started to look at that, and I started to realize that I did so much already, and I can continue for the long haul if needed.

Even just looking at this will help you stay positive and inspired. Most don't even realize how important this can be, and how just a little bit of inspiration can change your life, but it does. It really can mean a difference in the long haul, and it can make your life better and easier.

So yes, look for inspiration, look for all of the different ways you can better your home, and some of the different ways to organize yourself, and from there, you'll be able to change all of this and change your entire life for the positive.

Do this, and you'll see the difference that it makes not only in the current situation of how your space looks, but also, in the way your space looks later on.

Celebrating a New Home, a New Life

It goes without saying that once you've cleaned up your home, it will change your life. In most cases, you'll start to notice that the second you start putting everything together. You'll realize that it's easier to live life. The ease of life will make you happy, and it will make you feel good.

For most people, having the ease in place does make things a little bit better, as well. It'll allow for you to look at your space and see the truth of it, that it looks and feels better too.

Clean homes make you feel accomplished. Even if you do a little bit, it goes a long way.

If you clean up your home, take pictures along the way too.

This is a great way to make sure that you have the evidence of change. Whenever you feel down, pull out these photos. You'll see the difference, and how for you've come. Even over the year, if your project is a big one, you'll see the changes that you want to make. You'll be amazed at how different it can be for you, and how everything changes.

When you're cleaning your home, you will notice that when it comes to the process of cleaning it, it isn't fun, but it will help you see the potential that you've made so far. You can get a good feel for how far you've come, and how much you've accomplished by taking pictures and reporting progress.

The idea of seeing how far you've come in a clean home is a great way to inspire others to clean, and also will help you feel proud of the progress you've accomplished. For most people, they'll be able to feel inspired to get further with their progress. And it will help them to get a much better result from their activities, and build a better and cleaner home.

Start doing this today, figure out your motivation today, and you won't regret anything that you do.

CONCLUSION

Decluttering, cleaning, and organizing your home is most definitely possible. You have to go through the different steps to do it.

For those who are interested in decluttering, you learned everything that you need to know to declutter your home, from how to start handling all of the junk that you have. You also learned about the three piles, how they apply to the clutter you have lying about, and how you can, with just decluttering, have a much less messy space.

There is also the aspect of decluttering where you feel the sentiment for the items that you have. You'll realize as well that the sentimental feelings that you have for those items are just your brain trying to rationalize holding onto these things, and you'll realize as well that, once you start to clean up the space, you'll have a much happier, and healthier mindset too.

Organizing is something most people hate to do, simply because it takes a lot of effort to do, and you feel like you have to organize to the standard of one of those Good Housekeeping catalogs. But you don't. There are simple ways to make sure your space stays organized, and here, you've learned some of the optimal ways to make sure that you have the best organization possible, and you'll be able to, with this as well, understand that there are a lot of benefits to be had with this, and a lot that you can do with it.

For so many people, cleaning is the hardest part of this. Who likes cleaning anyways? Well, you don't have to suffer from the travails of cleaning anymore, and you'll be able to, with this book, have all the cleaning tools that you need, and you'll learn all of the quick and dirty ways to clean your stuff and maintain a happy space.

You'll be able to make sure that you get everyone nice and motivated as well. You should have fun with this, and we talked about how you can have a lot of fun with cleaning, and the best ways to ensure that you're cleaning and making an effort to bring forth some wonderful and amazing spaces that you'll feel proud of.

No longer do you have to spend your time setting down your items and forgetting them. You'll form habits that are invaluable and are fun to achieve. You'll realize that by doing this, you build a much healthier mindset, and you'll get your house cleaned up in no time. What many don't realize is how important it is to put this in place, and how, by just implementing all of these changes, you'll make a difference in no time.

Stop setting and forgetting it. Stop thinking that you have only a few minutes to do things and therefore you can't do anything about it. Instead, start to form different habitual activities that'll benefit you, and start to put forth a better, more rewarding process to help you ensure that you get the most out of this. Start to put together habits, and start cleaning and organizing your home, along with decluttering all of those troublesome spaces, today. You'll be grateful for this.

REFERENCES

Mique. (8 Feb. 2017). *Simple 15 minute a day cleaning schedule.* Retrieved from: https://www.thirtyhandmadedays.com/15-minute-day-cleaning-schedule/

10 Cleaning tools Everyone Should Own. Retrieved from: https://housewifehowtos.com/clean/10-cleaning-tools-everyone-should-own/

(27 Apr. 2018). Organize Your Storage Room with These 18 Decluttering Ideas. Retrieved from:

https://www.extraspace.com/blog/home-organization/room-organization/storage-room-organization-ideas-tips-to-declutter/

Jenn. *How to Declutter and Organize Any Space.* Retrieved from: https://www.cleanandscentsible.com/how-to-declutter-and-organize-any-space/

Michel, B. *The Stupid Simple Solution to Declutter Your Home and Keep It that Way.* Retrieved from: https://www.familyfelicity.com/simple-steps-declutter-home/

Babauta, L. *18 five-minute Decluttering Tips to Start Conquering Your Mess.* Retrieved from: https://zenhabits.net/18-five-minute-decluttering-tips-to-start-conquering-your-mess/

Amy. *Decluttering Paralysis: Strategies When you're Struggling to Declutter.* Retrieved from: https://organizationboutique.com/decluttering-paralysis/

Kaplan, J. (3 Nov. 2019). *7 Reasons to Declutter Rooms.* Retrieved from: https://www.thespruce.com/reasons-to-declutter-right-now-4140438

Ongaro, A. *5 Ways to Start Decluttering Today!).* Retrieved from: https://www.breakthetwitch.com/start-decluttering/

How to Organize Storage Rooms. Retrieved from: https://homeguides.sfgate.com/organize-storage-rooms-54201.html

Baginski, K. and Miller, M. (27 Feb. 2019). *15 Quick Tips for Keeping an Organized Kitchen.* Retrieved from: https://www.hgtv.com/design/rooms/kitchens/quick-tips-for-keeping-an-organized-kitchen-pictures

Pinksky, S. *The Ultimate Room-By-Room Organization Guide.* Retrieved from: https://www.additudemag.com/slideshows/how-to-organize-your-home-room-by-room/

Nystul, J. (24 Jun. 2014). *A Step-by-Step Guide to a Clean Kitchen.*

Retrieved from: https://www.onegoodthingbyjillee.com/step-step-clean-kitchen/